N. D. C.
OPERATIONS
INFORMATION
UNIT 12/3/99

Universities and the Creation of Wealth

SRHE and Open University Press Imprint
General Editor: Heather Eggins

Current titles include:

Catherine Bargh, Peter Scott and David Smith: *Governing Universities*
Ronald Barnett: *Improving Higher Education: Total Quality Care*
Ronald Barnett: *The Idea of Higher Education*
Ronald Barnett: *The Limits of Competence*
Ronald Barnett: *Higher Education: A Critical Business*
John Bird: *Black Students and Higher Education*
Jean Bocock and David Watson (eds): *Managing the Curriculum*
David Boud *et al.* (eds): *Using Experience for Learning*
Angela Brew (ed.): *Directions in Staff Development*
Anne Brockbank and Ian McGill: *Facilitating Reflective Learning in Higher Education*
Ann Brooks: *Academic Women*
Sally Brown and Angela Glasner (eds): *Assessment Matters in Higher Education*
Robert G. Burgess (ed.): *Beyond the First Degree*
Frank Coffield and Bill Williamson (eds): *Repositioning Higher Education*
John Cowan: *On Becoming an Innovative University Teacher*
Rob Cuthbert (ed.): *Working in Higher Education*
Heather Eggins (ed.): *Women as Leaders and Managers in Higher Education*
G.R. Evans: *Calling Academia to Account*
David Farnham (ed.): *Managing Academic Staff in Changing University Systems*
Sinclair Goodlad: *The Quest for Quality*
Harry Gray (ed.): *Universities and the Creation of Wealth*
Diana Green (ed.): *What is Quality in Higher Education?*
Robin Middlehurst: *Leading Academics*
Sarah Neal: *The Making of Equal Opportunities Policies in Universities*
David Palfreyman and David Warner (eds): *Higher Education and the Law*
Moira Peelo: *Helping Students with Study Problems*
John Pratt: *The Polytechnic Experiment*
Michael Prosser and Keith Trigwell: *Understanding Learning and Teaching*
Tom Schuller (ed.): *The Changing University?*
Peter Scott (ed.): *The Globalization of Higher Education*
Peter Scott: *The Meanings of Mass Higher Education*
Harold Silver and Pamela Silver: *Students*
Anthony Smith and Frank Webster (eds): *The Postmodern University?*
Imogen Taylor: *Developing Learning in Professional Education*
Paul R. Trowler: *Academics Responding to Change*
David Warner and Elaine Crosthwaite (eds): *Human Resource Management in Higher and Further Education*
David Warner and Charles Leonard: *The Income Generation Handbook* (Second Edition)
David Warner and David Palfreyman (eds): *Higher Education Management*
Graham Webb: *Understanding Staff Development*
Sue Wheeler and Jan Birtle: *A Handbook for Personal Tutors*

Universities and the Creation of Wealth

Edited by
Harry Gray

The Society for Research into Higher Education
& Open University Press

Published by SRHE and
Open University Press
Celtic Court
22 Ballmoor
Buckingham
MK18 1XW

email: enquiries@openup.co.uk
world wide web: http://www.openup.co.uk

and
325 Chestnut Street
Philadelphia, PA 19106, USA

First Published 1999

Copyright © The editor and contributors 1999

All rights reserved. Except for the quotation of short passages for the purpose of criticism and review, no part of this publication may be reproduced, stored in a retrieval system, or transmitted, in any form or by any means, electronic, mechanical, photocopying, recording or otherwise, without the prior written permission of the publisher or a licence from the Copyright Licensing Agency Limited. Details of such licences (for reprographic reproduction) may be obtained from the Copyright Licensing Agency Ltd of 90 Tottenham Court Road, London, W1P 9HE.

A catalogue record of this book is available from the British Library

ISBN 0 335 20309 4 (pbk)   0 335 20133 4 (hbk)

Library of Congress Cataloging-in-Publication Data
Universities and the creation of wealth / edited by Harry Gray.
    p.   cm.
  Includes bibliographical references and index.
  ISBN 0-335-20133-4. — ISBN 0-335-20309-4 (pbk.)
  1. Education, Higher—Economic aspects—Great Britain—Case studies. 2. Education, Higher—Economic aspects—Canada.
3. Education, Higher—Economic aspects—Asia, Southeastern.
4. Education, Higher—Social aspects—Great Britain—Case studies.
5. Education, Higher—Social aspects—Canada. 6. Education, Higher—Social aspects—Asia, Southeastern, I. Gray, H.L.
LC67.68.G7U52   1999
338.4'3378—dc21
                                          98-19449
                                              CIP

Typeset by Graphicraft Limited, Hong Kong
Printed in Great Britain by St Edmundsbury Press Ltd, Bury St Edmunds, Suffolk

Contents

Contributors	vii
Foreword	xi
Sir Geoffrey Holland	
Preface	xiii
Harry Gray	

Part 1   A New Awareness 1
Introduction 1
Harry Gray
 1 Re-scoping the University 3
    Harry Gray
 2 Knowledge Societies, Intellectual Capital and
    Economic Growth 18
    David Robertson
 3 How Universities Can Thrive Locally in a Global Economy 36
    John Goddard
 4 Measuring the Economic Impact of Universities: Canada 47
    Marc Trudeau and Fernand Martin
 5 The Changing Relationship Between Higher Education
    and Small and Medium Sized Enterprises 66
    Martin Binks
 6 The Role of Universities in Economic Growth:
    the ASEAN Countries 80
    Paul Milne

Part 2   Examples and Cases 93
Introduction 93
Harry Gray
 7 Universities and Communities: Cases from North-East
    England 95
    Derek Fraser

8	The Impact of a New University on its Community: the University of Warwick *Michael Shattock*	109
9	Salford University: an Historical Industrial Partnership *Peter Brandon*	123
10	The University of Sheffield's Regional Office: Forging Relationships Between a Traditional Civic University and its Regional Community *Marilyn Wedgwood and Brigitte Pemberton*	141
11	Towards the Community University *Harry Gray*	150

Index	158
The Society for Research into Higher Education	165

Contributors

Martin Binks is a senior lecturer at the University of Nottingham specializing in entrepreneurship and the financing of small and medium sized enterprises (SMEs). A visiting professor at the Claremont Graduate School in California he works with several UK government departments such as the Department for Education and Employment (DfEE) and the Department of Trade and Industry (DTI). A council member of the Small Business Research Trust, he is involved in the creation of an East Midlands Business Barometer which aims to build more effective links between higher education, local business support agencies and SMEs.

Peter Brandon is Pro-Vice-Chancellor for Research and Graduate Studies at the University of Salford where he heads the Research and Graduate College encompassing six multidisciplinary research institutes and the graduate school. He has initiated several national research centres at Salford in conjunction with industry and in his own research has worked with over 20 firms in the construction industry. In the UK he chaired the Science and Engineering Research Council (SERC) Construction Committee for five years and was chairman of the Research Assessment Exercise for the Built Environment and Town Planning Panels in 1996.

Derek Fraser is Vice-Chancellor of the University of Teesside. He was formerly one of Her Majesty's Inspectors (HMI) in the further and higher education sector.

John Goddard is Head of the Centre for Urban and Regional Studies at the University of Newcastle upon Tyne. He is author of the Committee of Vice-chancellors and Principals' (CVCP) report *Universities and their Communities* and has recently undertaken a lengthy study for the DfEE of the role universities play in regional economies.

Harry Gray, editor of this volume, is Visiting Professor in Strategic Leadership at the University of Salford and was for nine years a higher education adviser to the DfEE. He has written extensively on education and management and is a leading figure in the European Network for Innovation and Learning in Organizations and the Community (ENILOC). He is a director of MES which runs The WISDOM Project, which is concerned with improving the economic contribution of older workers to sustaining national wealth.

Sir Geoffrey Holland is Vice-Chancellor of the University of Exeter. He was previously permanent secretary in the Employment Department Group and then in the Department for Education. In 1977 he published the government report *Young People and Work*, which was highly regarded. He had a major part in the development of the Training and Enterprise Councils. He played a key role in the setting up of the Enterprise in Higher Education initiative which has been the most potent force for change in the higher education curriculum this century.

Fernand Martin received his PhD from McGill University in 1961. Since then he has taught at the University of Manitoba, the University of Saskatchewan and McGill University. He is currently *Professeur Titulaire* in the department of economics at the University of Montreal, Canada.

Paul Milne is a senior lecturer in economics at the University of Hull where he teaches in the newly-formed Institute for Learning. He also teaches regularly in the Association of South East Asian Nations (ASEAN) countries and has a broad experience of business education.

Brigitte Pemberton worked for 14 years in economic development for Sheffield City Council in a senior management position and recently took up her present post as Assistant Director at the Sheffield University Regional Office. She has travelled extensively as an economic development consultant in Eastern Europe.

David Robertson is Professor of Public Policy and Education at Liverpool John Moores University. He is currently undertaking research for the DfEE into higher education and the international labour market. He is author of two research appendices to the Dearing Report – on wider participation for students from working class backgrounds (Report 6) and on new funding options (Report 13). He is also author of the wide-ranging 'Robertson Report', *Choosing to Change*, a major government-sponsored review of student choice and mobility in further and higher education.

Michael Shattock is Registrar of the University of Warwick. His two most recent books are *The UGC and the Management of British Universities* (1994) and *The Creation of a University System* (1997). He is also the editor of the journal *Minerva*.

Marc Trudeau received his masters degree in economics from the University of Western Ontario in 1995. He is currently a senior policy analyst with the Association of Universities and Colleges of Canada. His portfolio includes research on Canada's national system of innovation and the impacts of university research.

Marilyn Wedgwood set up the regional office of the University of Sheffield under the direction of the vice-chancellor to stimulate a stronger interaction between the university and the community for mutual benefit. Previously she was director of enterprise in higher education at Sheffield and now works throughout Yorkshire and the Humber to develop alliances and partnerships in order to generate effective and meaningful modes of interaction. New European Regional Development Fund (ERDF) projects are underway to bring business sectors into closer association with the university.

Foreword

Sir Geoffrey Holland

Higher education is the great, largely unknown and certainly underexploited resource contributing to the creation of wealth and economic competitiveness. Many outside higher education still do not recognize the capacity of that resource or how to get at it, and many of those inside higher education do not know how best to connect with the world outside. It is much more than seeking research contracts from the commercial or industrial sectors. It is much more than graduating increasing numbers of young people and mature students. It is about coming to grips with, and contributing to, a new world.

That said, higher education has always made a very substantial contribution. Its research has underpinned some of the most successful and important technological and other advances. Its graduates – until now a minority of any age group – have been leaders in industry, commerce and government. Many of the offerings of higher education – and far more than many people give credit for – are vocational in orientation. Even so, higher education has done little more than scratch the surface of the contributions it could make.

The report of the National Committee of Enquiry into the Future of Higher Education (the Dearing Report) has made it timely to re-examine the contribution of higher education and to address the challenge and opportunities that lie ahead as we enter a new century and new millennium. Are the offerings of higher education preparing young people adequately for that century? Is there sufficiently wide access and sufficiently wide choice of time and mode of learning? Is higher education recognizing sufficiently the expectations of students young and old, part-time or full-time, in jobs or not? Are there sufficient opportunities in any local community? Is there sufficient innovation and are standards sufficiently rigorous and set sufficiently high? However much they have already done, universities have barely begun to make the contribution they could to wealth creation and economic development in local communities, to technology transfer, to working with the world outside their boundaries. Even in departments of business studies or management, the changing needs of small and medium sized firms, of new employment patterns, of portfolio lives, of the entrepreneur, have barely begun to be addressed.

Higher education is still a giant who is only half awake. If higher education has been and is about anything it is about exploiting and realizing the potential of the world around us and understanding it better. That world is full of people (a fact that universities do not always seem to remember) and one thing that we know for sure is that the potential of individuals in this country – or any other – has never been fully realized. Universities need to send out a clear message to the people and to those who employ them that they understand their needs and the opportunities, are committed to achievement in partnership with them, have the means and know the way, and also have the will.

This book shows clearly what can be done and what has yet to be done. It is an important contribution to what must be a vital new phase in the history of higher education.

Preface

Harry Gray

Those of us who have travelled widely in British higher education (HE) in recent years are aware of how great the changes are that have occurred. The basis has been laid for even greater changes in the purposes of HE and the structures which will support it. There is talk internationally of the 'massification' of HE but the change is more than just an increase in volume; it is one of function. Until the Second World War, HE in its university form was an élitist experience. However, as the grammar schools began to steer pupils from a wider social background into university, HE became increasingly the way into the professions. Quite quickly it became a middle-class expectation that, after school, university would be the best preparation for employment in a respectable job. But there has always been a strong view that HE is of limited usefulness; that for many people it is not suitable.

This is because for most people (and most academics) university is perceived as the third stage of education within a tightly controlled system – hence the idea of A levels as gold standard. There are many pressures now for extension beyond the broad élite of 35 per cent of the age group not because it is thought that a broader range of students will benefit but because as HE becomes more useful there are more occasions when its usefulness can be extended. If we want to see the future for universities we need only look at the margins, where we can observe that many more people believe they have a right to benefit from what universities do. Nowadays every English county wants its own university, although there are very few left without one. Many further education (FE) institutions aspire to offer some courses at HE level and many large companies are seized with the idea of setting up universities of their own.

Does this mean that the appetite for university education is growing? Perhaps not for the kind of university education that has been available in the past – institutional and college confined – but for university education as it might become. There is in fact a wholly new spirit abroad in British HE that is more democratic and more demotic than has been the case in the past. There is a strong belief that universities have something that can and ought to be shared with other players and other people. Often there is no understanding of what that mysterious quality might be but it has something to do with the intellectual capital that universities develop and sustain and which can be applied elsewhere. The interest is in using what universities have to offer even when academics are unwilling to declare their activity to be mundanely useful.

After a slow start the UK polytechnics – now retitled universities – have begun to look back at their original purposes and discover that they have a practical role in society. Not only are they there to help people to learn how to work more effectively (and raise their personal standard of living and quality of life) but they can contribute to the capability of commerce and industry and thereby enhance the general economic good. There is at the present time something of a sea change in academia but clearly in the spirit of the age. Gradually the other-worldliness of HE is being brought down to earth and universities are engaging with real people and real problems.

One of the major consequences of this change is that universities are opening up to new clients. Not only are they working more closely with companies and firms, businesses and institutions, but they are looking for new kinds of learner in new kinds of situation. No longer is the typical student aged between 18 and 21 or 24; the whole age range of lifelong learning is looking to universities to offer something useful and exciting. Adult education has left its backwater of evening classes and is moving through continuing professional development via continuing vocational education and training in marginal departments to being mainstreamed as the core business of professionally-orientated departments where traditional disciplines are taught.

The universities are becoming new places doing new things in new ways with new people. All the changes are not yet visible but in this book some of them are described, the principles on which change is occurring are outlined and some of the visions are anticipated. The theme of the book seemed somewhat rarefied when it was first thought about but already it has become almost core thinking – that universities have a positive economic role to play in partnership with all the other participants in economic and social development. Hopefully, the timeliness of the book will be noted and many more academics will respond to the needs of the outside world. Universities are a largely untapped resource in many areas of material and spiritual life. This can no longer be allowed to remain the case.

We should begin to look more closely – and academics behind their learned walls would be advised to do this quickly – at the kinds of shift that are already taking place in HE. There is perhaps more thinking about the purpose and structure of HE outside the universities than within them, particularly in international companies such as Ford Motors and Microsoft. One can detect an impatience outside HE with academics and their often self-centred, institution-biased thinking. There is a growth of interest in other than traditional forms of university exemplified by such projected schemes as the Higher Education Centre of Mansfield, the Swindon University project and the thinking about the University of Cumbria (the University of the Lakes). These are less likely to follow the model of the University of the Highlands which is after all a traditional form, like the Open University, that uses modern telematic mechanisms for course delivery. Stockton College, although under the wing of one of Britain's most traditional and conservative universities (Durham), is developing new ways of thinking about HE and new forms of cooperation with FE and employers in the area. The University for Industry gives us a chance to rethink the idea in terms of a community university and there are likely to be more changes in the forms of delivery as modern information technology (IT) comes into greater dominance in the home.

But perhaps the most concrete and mind-concentrating development in the UK will be the appearance of overseas universities – led by the Americans – recruiting UK students for highly attractive, well resourced and imaginative courses that have enticing financial loan deals attached to them. There is also the possibility that European institutions will latch on to the possibility of recruiting in the UK (as the business schools already do), and many firms who are prepared to pay fees in exchange for first refusal for recruitment will be happy to arrange for tuition in the best locations by unit or module. UK universities may not be best favoured in these processes unless they rethink themselves in terms of the balance between research and teaching. One of the characteristics, even of the entrepreneurial universities in the UK, is that the likelihood of foreign competition is seldom considered. But in a new age of worldwide HE we have hardly begun to envisage the changes that are on the horizon.

Part 1

A New Awareness

Introduction

It is only in comparatively recent years that universities have begun to take seriously their positive role in sustaining and developing the national economy. For most of their history universities had taken it for granted that their very presence was for the general benefit of the nation. After all, they produced highly qualified graduates, engaged in research at the forefront of invention and provided jobs galore in their local community as well as a great deal of local purchasing power.

One of the effects of the utilitarian politics of the 1980s was to cause a closer examination of what universities actually do. It was found, for example, that the graduates they produced were not as well prepared for the workplace as they might be. It was also realized that the universities were more dependent than they had admitted on business and industry, not only for funding but for ideas. Universities also found themselves competing more intensely among themselves for funds and resources.

The UK polytechnics had always considered themselves to be vocational institutions but 'academic drift' – which still continues – made them less self-regarding about their economic purposes and they often hankered after a more rarefied form of academic prestige. On the other hand, some of the longer-established universities – some of the quite old ones like Manchester and newer ones like Warwick – had begun to take their relationship with business and industry a lot more seriously.

In Part 1 the writers explore the general ideas that accompany the new thinking about universities as positive economic engines for change and raise issues about how far this new thinking has to go and what its nature is. At the present time a great deal of thought is being given to the role of universities in their regional communities. This is bolstered in the UK by the imminent establishment of Regional Development Agencies (RDAs) and the declared intention of the university funding councils to take regional issues into consideration when determining funding.

Universities are, of course, only loosely coupled systems and it is necessary to look at what they do at the level of departments rather than the institutional level. It has become clear that the strength of economic performance in universities lies in what individuals do within their departments, and this is often not known at the institutional level and certainly not by outside bodies such as government departments.

The economic role of universities will continue to undergo changes and development. There will undoubtedly be new concepts of what a university is and how its services should be delivered. As with many social changes those who lead and those who follow are far apart and just as some are catching up others are changing yet again. If greater equality of support for part-time students is realized then the whole environment of HE will be transformed. There is a space here that will be well worth watching.

1
Re-scoping the University

Harry Gray

A reorientation

The most remarkable but undernoted change in British universities over the last 15 years or so has been a recognition that they have a role to play in the development of local economies (Goddard 1994; McNicholl 1997). While academics are as insistent as ever that they have an international role as well as a national one, many have taken to looking closely at how they might be involved in local and community matters in their capacity as researchers and consultants. In many ways this is a legacy of the polytechnics but nowadays some of the more traditional universities such as the great civics (Liverpool, Manchester, Sheffield, Leeds etc.) cherish their local role. Some (like Salford and Warwick) even glory in it and others are somewhat disappointed that there is no large industrial presence with which they might interact professionally (Kent at Canterbury for example). Universities are often proud that they make a contribution to local cash flows by virtue of their simply being there, but more and more they are beginning to recognize that they can play a positive and proactive rather than a negative and dependent role within the local economy and their domestic catchment area. The development of this new perspective provides the substance of this chapter.

A continually changing state

Universities as organizations are not as well understood as many people – including academics – think (Ferlie *et al.* 1996). Not only is there great diversity of practice within them – partly a consequence of their varied origins – but there is a great variance in the kinds of social coherence within them. In the popular imagination the archetypal UK universities are Oxford and Cambridge (elided into Oxbridge in common parlance) but they are typical neither of one another nor any other university. The forms of management vary enormously and lie on the polarity from efficient to incompetent as well as other poles such as collegial–authoritarian, organic–mechanistic, technological–liberal arts and so on. Universities are virtually ignored in the literature of management and organization theory even though most writers on management work in universities (Bess 1984; Ferlie *et al.* 1996). There are a few studies by higher education (HE) practitioners (such as Lockwood and Davies 1985; Middlehurst 1993) but they are sparse and somewhat inward-looking. Yet as we approach the end of the millennium the change activity in universities is as great as in any industry anywhere else, and closer studies would be rewarding not least for the insights they would provide for managing other kinds of organization. While education is one of the great genres of organization it is also the most isolated and overlooked.

Nothing in UK HE will be quite the same again after the reports from the committees looking at FE and HE – Dearing (1997) and Kennedy (1997b) – and the government Green Paper on adult education following the Fryer Report (Fryer 1997). But the changes had already begun even before the government began to take a serious interest, and the ground was well prepared for a sea change. All the ideas in these reports had been well canvassed and discussed, though since those who work in HE are not used to anticipating forced change the reports were preceded by much discussion but little tangible preparation. As is usual with organizational and institutional change, the origins of change always form outside the system (Schön 1973; Senge 1994) and make their impact through material causes – financial, economic, demographic, political or whatever. On the whole, organizations – and institutions especially – prefer not to change unless change is forced upon them; only the most competitive organizations anticipate changes in demand (that is, within their market or environment) and take positive action to accommodate those changes. Perhaps that is why the universities have actually done very little in practice to anticipate likely government reforms of HE.

What are universities?

The fact that universities have been little written about except for the most part in romantic terms (Newman 1961 and any number of novels) and have not received much attention from organization theorists (Bess 1984) leaves us with a poor theoretical basis for understanding them, and we have to fall back on descriptive and historical perspectives (Gray 1995) in an attempt to understand what universities are and what they might become. The idea of the university as somehow detached from the hurly-burly of ordinary life is strong in the academic imagination. Many university teachers – even those in the most vocationally-orientated universities – like to dream of colleges set in peaceful scholarly havens away from the madding crowds where reading and thinking are the primary activities. More than 95 per cent of universities are not like this and never will be, and those that are did not begin in this way since the medieval university was composed of itinerant scholars who went where they could find patrons, students and material support.

It is easy to imagine a perfect university as a place where scholars just sit and think and if money were no object it is likely there would be some of these around. But since such places do not exist it is probable that something more is required of them than intellectual self-indulgence. The reality of universities is that they serve functional purposes and depend on funding with conditions attached – and rather large sums of 'unearned' funding at that. This means that they are forced to function within an academic market-place with all the characteristics of any other open market. The tradition for all universities (except for a very few in the Arab world) depends on both public and private funding of various kinds. In their attempts to gain more funds and to please the sources of these funds, all universities have become increasingly more concerned with being perceived as being 'relevant' to the needs of funders. Invariably these requirements are economic in one way or another and they certainly have costs.

Formative considerations

The majority of universities in the UK were in fact established to fulfil economic functions. That meant they were intended to further the local development of trade and industry and to enhance the capability of members of the professions (new and historic). The federal civic Victoria University of Manchester, Liverpool, Leeds, Birmingham and Sheffield was based on local institutions such as Manchester's Owens College which were founded for just such economic purposes. Salford was founded as a college of commerce and technology for the same reason. As the original Salford charter states, the new institution will 'prepare students for capability in the workplace' through 'drawing of inputs from industry, commerce, the public sector and the professions, developing problem and research-based learning methods, and extending the opportunity for integrated work experience and training' (quoted in Carboni *et al.* 1996: 1).

The first signs that universities might have to change to deal with a different student population other than youngsters straight from school came with the first wave of mature students after the Second World War (Kermode 1997) but their basic purpose was not questioned. It was only with the establishment of new universities, following on from the emergency teacher training colleges, that institutional change began to take place that took as a concern the professional development of young people for economic purposes.

The new post-war universities – along with the Colleges of Advanced Technology (CATs) which soon became technical universities, and the somewhat anomalous University of Keele – were all founded to supply graduates to fill the growing need for more highly trained professionals, while the polytechnics were set up to enhance the quality of those working in technical fields. All universities were organized on the basis of full-time undergraduate degree courses, on the unquestioning assumption that a university degree marked professional and technical vocational competency at a similar level. It is the largely uncritical acceptance of a full-time university first degree as the determinant of the basic organizational structure for any university that has been the biggest factor in preventing other and more appropriate forms of HE from developing. (In secondary education something of the same effect has been caused by the uncritical belief that A levels offer a valid gold standard for all secondary school education.) This is true even of those 'new' universities (such as Central Lancashire and Oxford Brookes) whose first degrees are entirely modular with a considerable element of free choice.

Universities have twisted and turned around their basic preoccupation with first degrees, and increased the relevance of university education to both occupational and vocational education and training. The forces compelling them towards a practical orientation have not only been the funding mechanisms of the various and successive funding bodies but also a growth in rhetoric from the employing sector for students to be 'better prepared for working life' – the reason for Enterprise in Higher Education (EHE) (Gray 1995). Since the mid-1980s the move towards vocationalism everywhere in education has known no bounds (Skilbeck et al. 1994) and some of the new universities have been able to centre their development not only on occupational and vocational training but also on a well-defined and purposefully directed local (sub-regional) concern. By the end of the century the polarity among universities (or sections within them) will be such that at one end there will be almost complete orientation towards the locality while at the other the concern will be for virtual transnationality and locational disembodiment. In Canada examples are the University of Waterloo with its strong local commitment while at the other pole is the Ivey School of Business which sees itself as having to out-Harvard Harvard in its global orientation. In the UK the poles are presented by Teesside as against Durham (with the interesting case of Stockton College in the middle[1]) or Lancaster as against Central Lancashire. The creation of a new university currently under consideration in Cumbria, however, would be for the purpose of creating a vehicle for sub-regional economic regeneration and might well be an example of a new kind of university altogether. The University of the Highlands and Islands, however, appears to have depended on a simpler and more traditional way of thinking about universities as passive centres of economic activity.

Irreconcilable?

One of the important questions about change in HE is whether two conflicting concepts – local or transnational – are totally reconcilable. The answer depends on finding alternative approaches to the increasingly incompatible core activities of teaching and research. Just as universities have a basic structure based on the full-time undergraduate degree (be it three years or four, sandwich or continuous) so the workload of academics is required to carry both teaching and research commitments. On the whole, universities that have not had the courage to declare themselves essentially vocational (as have, for the most part, the former polytechnics) experience a tension between research and teaching with research being much more highly valued and rewarded than teaching. Research in this context means 'theoretical' research as against the applied research the former polytechnics like to engage in. This conflict reached a notorious and discreditable point in 1997 when the University of Nottingham tried to offload staff who did not have a good enough record in theoretical research. Eventually the matter was resolved with little loss of face on either side but the reason for the collision was the impact of the research assessment exercise that the English funding council engaged in. In this exercise universities are graded for their performance in research and the good departments are rewarded with extra funding. This causes a tension for lecturers who wish to engage in teaching (for which the students pay directly) rather than research (for which the research and funding councils pay). Clearly research is valued more highly than teaching even though research has never been the main income-generating activity of universities.

To have two equally important core activities makes organizational nonsense (even though it is claimed that the quality of teaching depends on the quality of research – a contention that has never been proved). The important consequence for this chapter is that in putting energy into trying to reconcile two incompatible demands, many universities have been unable to give their attention to fulfilling a proactive economic role. Through the funding system for British universities since the Second World War universities have existed managerially in a state of total dependency. The funding body has performed all the strategic tasks for HE (policy, strategy, funding ratios, even the allocation of subjects to institutions) and the universities simply follow a lead and a direction that they have no real choice of avoiding. In any case, British universities have never been strategically-led institutions and self-determination only began to occur in the early 1990s when additional discretionary funds became available – project funding from government departments, the European Union (EU), the Training and Enterprise Councils (TECs) and other economically-orientated government agencies. The government department which might have been expected to have some influence on changing the curriculum – the Department of Education and Science (DES) – took no interest at all in what went on inside universities (though there had been an HM Inspectorate for the polytechnics) and it was only after the Employment Department and the Department of Education and Science were amalgamated in 1994 that the Employment Department's interest in vocational HE became of any interest to the professional education civil servants in the new Department for Education and Employment (DfEE).

In the traditional universities, research achievement is still the basic condition for promotion and involvement with the employing sector – that actually recruits students – has stayed at arm's length. The nature of this difference can be seen by comparing, for example, Salford, Warwick and Cranfield with any of the old civic universities. At these three universities an emphasis on applied research as against pure research has led to close involvement and partnership with industry and commerce, while a strong emphasis on vocational training has meant that graduates have no difficulty in finding employment. Of course, they have not gone far enough if the idea of a university is reconceptualized as being a place of positive economic activity rather than just academic reflection, but their cases show that progress can be made even when funding regimes are not adequately thought out. If universities had a clearer basis for their existence some of the more erratic and eccentric episodes of maverick managerial behaviour (such as that which is supposed to have occurred recently at Huddersfield and Lancaster) would have been unlikely and they would have developed a clarity of purpose that would lend coherence to their sometimes erratic planning.

Concentrating corporate minds

In spite of a host of strong influences against change, universities have in the last 15 years or so made remarkable strides towards playing a more proactive role in their social and economic environments – localities, subregions, and regions as well as nationally and internationally. It could be argued that the business schools (in fact they were often 'management' schools in spite of their titles) were in the forefront of developments that had an essentially skills-development function; after all the Manchester and London Business Schools were founded just for the purpose of improving the quality of British management. Elsewhere vocational and occupational interests, though still at the heart of their purpose (such as textiles in Lancashire and Yorkshire or engineering in Birmingham and Sheffield), were victims of the decline in their industries. The universities largely followed this decline and closed their departments in preference to working at the provision of alternatives. The irony is that these great expensive institutions, economically significant in terms of local spending power, were not equipped to draw on their intellectual capital or financial muscle to assist in the regeneration of their regions. If the government provided special funding they would spend it – then ask for more – but few of them saw it as their responsibility to become a generative resource for economic renewal. If there is any significant cause for criticism of the British university system it is that it has been unwilling to take responsibility for itself in an age of economic growth. Yet if one were to be looking for the key economic engines in any area after the decline of the major industries, those engines would be the health service, local government and education. In some areas (north Lancashire for example) there are no major industries *other* than local government, the health service and HE.

Economic engines

The central theme of this chapter is that universities are (it would be nice to write 'have been') the great missing factor in regional economic renewal and indeed of the whole country's economic development. Clearly academics have been hugely active in advisory capacities and as researchers to government departments, industry and commerce. But this has been an activity of individuals and sub-departments, not of faculties and universities as a whole. Indeed, consultancy has been the great hidden area of university activity largely because it has been pursued mostly by individuals in a private capacity. Only very recently has consultancy been written into contracts or a financial share drawn back to the university. As economic engines, universities have been woefully underpowered and often wilfully neglectful of what could be considered their basic obligations. In the 1990s there was a spate of papers and reports endeavouring to show how much universities contributed to their local economy, but in this capacity they were portrayed as neutral or even negative players in economic and social activity (see, for example, Bleaney *et al.* 1992; Greater Manchester Universities 1995; Dearing 1997, Appendix 9). This is even true of the Committee of Vice-chancellors and Principals' (CVCP) report, *The Impact of Universities and Colleges on the UK Economy* (McNicholl 1997). Reports such as these showed how much spending power the universities brought to an area through student recruitment and through employment not only of academics (national recruitment) but of lay workers (local recruitment of cleaners, janitors, groundsmen and tradesmen). There is no doubt that some of the so-called 'new' universities (not ex-polytechnics) like York, Bath, Norwich and Lancaster were founded with the hope of positive economic benefit to the area, but they were nevertheless conceived on traditional university principles and not, like the polytechnics, on models of vocational education.

If the core business of a university – of whatever origins – is the development of 'intellectual capital' (to use Michael Shattock's felicitous phrase, personal communication) then there are many more creative and versatile ways of doing this than by simply running three-year full-time undergraduate degrees and expecting lecturers to spend as much time as possible doing research of the sort favoured by the research councils with their old-style university research values. (Even the Open University is basically organized round a traditional degree structure with its conventional assumptions about how learning occurs.) Many of the new universities knew this even if they were in practice making the best of a bad job. Some of the older universities also knew this, at least in some of their parts. Salford was faced with financial catastrophe, and Warwick was challenged by its inceptual disadvantages, while others such as Teesside and Derby made advantage out of necessity. In fact, Derby and Teesside began with a narrow academic base and very local reputation, so they had to fight hard to gain respectable reputations as 'universities'. But on the whole universities have been more concerned with their own growth and development than that of the communities in which they are located. Indeed, some of them exist as almost independent social entities with all their own facilities such as shops, banks, pubs and entertainment. But having said this, the changes brought about by new sources of funding (such as European money of various kinds) have enabled some of them to reorientate a great deal and all of them to change their perspective on society in some measure.

Marginal activity

None of this is intended to denigrate the activity undertaken by a wide range of individuals and units within the institutions. The former polytechnics were very good at tailoring their activities to suit external customers, but for such purposes they tended to use additional funding or charge special rates to the customer. Funds arising from this activity have come to be known as 'marginal money' because they are independent of core and continuing funding. The number of small marginal operations dealing with external customers direct is legion. One of the commonest forms is industrial liaison which draws on much Department of Trade and Industry (DTI) and Department of the Environment money. Other forms of involvement are industry-linked, whereby the institution undertakes contract research or course provision. In some cases, large companies such as British Airways and Rover Motors buy custom-built whole degree courses. Furthermore, there is a vast amount of purchasing of courses by individuals at masters and doctorate levels where companies pay the fees and expenses of employees to gain further professional development. Over the last 15–20 years such bespoke provision has proliferated following the success of the business schools in drawing in full-cost funds from customers and clients.

However, none of this has seriously affected the view of most senior management in universities that the core and serious business of their institutions is research of international calibre and the teaching of undergraduate courses. One effect of this is that some units working at the graduate level have separated from their parent universities and many more have contemplated it (drawing back perhaps at the thought of having to generate their own total income in perpetuity). Cranfield is probably the one exception within the state system; Buckingham the sole instance outside it. Business schools have an uncertain relationship with the parent organization; sometimes they want to be in and sometimes they want to be out. The basic problem with the traditional view of the institutions is that it is based on the delivery of content (facts and opinions) rather than learning processes. And the control of content is the arbitrary choice of individual academics or their professional associations rather than the real-life needs of people who work in economic organizations.

The problem has become particularly acute in medicine where there is in place a new view of the learning process based on problem solving and the practical application of research. Sadly, the kind of research most valued by the funding bodies is theoretical (blue skies) research, not applied research. Universities are trying to move towards high ratings in pure research in order to attract additional funds, albeit in effect marginal ones. Thus there is a tension between what organizations in the economic world outside universities want and what universities themselves want and reward. Yet it would seem to the outside observer that if a university were to be engaged in doing research that relates to local usefulness, that research would thereby (by virtue of its usefulness) be eminently transferable and applicable elsewhere, especially globally. There seems here to be an unresolved issue in academia worldwide: can it really be the case that universities should compete against one another – rather than cooperate – in world terms on matters which have little relevance to the needs of business and industry, society and social institutions, health and medicine, local and national government etc.? Of course not. Everyone can recognize the need for applied and theoretical research but it does seem to have got sadly mixed up within the institutions and within the various national and international systems.

An answer

Until the matter of a degree as an artefact has been resolved there will be no great progress. The nub of the problem is that universities actually gain their public prestige and income by being validating bodies. That is, they give a seal of approval (degree, diploma or certificate) and it is this that they sell in the market and this which people buy. Universities are very protective of this legally enforced right; if any old body were able to award degrees, the universities might find a dearth of customers. So for the most part customers have little choice. If you want to go to university you have to go there to get a degree (preferably a 'good' one). If you don't get a degree then your activity has been of second best quality however useful it might be to you outside – in getting a job, for instance. But why cannot customers buy what they want? You can go to a department store and buy a tie without having to buy a whole outfit, or to a supermarket without taking up any of the 'best buy' offers, so why not have a personal choice at a university? Some academics will abhor the commercial terms such as customer, market, buy, etc. but universities owe their existence to financial transactions. They are not free of bargaining relations (though they might like to be) and they are increasingly bound by the legal restraints that surround contracts. Once universities are able to offer their intellectual capital for use through negotiated processes that are valid for the customers, they will be able to contribute much more effectively to the national economy that provides the funding for their existing research and teaching.

In an age of changing demands for HE, universities need to vary the nature of their 'product' and look to finding new kinds of relationships with their customers and clients. They can do this by engaging in new kinds of partnership and collaborative processes. The universities will always have an edge on most other organizations in the breadth and depth of their intellectual capital. Their only rivals will be the specialist companies that need to keep ahead of discovery through innovation, which necessitates that they support laboratories and product development functions – pharmacy, electronics and engineering are outstanding examples. However, even here, university staff play a leading role as consultants and advisers. Such collaboration means that people have to work together, often in groups and teams – the classical research mode. Such ways of working are not strange to academics since both research and teaching can occur in a collaborative discovery mode. But working like this is not like lecturing to large classes, examining with trick questions, or grading people's performance on a subjective (falsely objective) basis. Of course, having to lecture to very large classes is one of the justified gripes of lecturers but it is a problem of their own making because of the traditional manner in which they have insisted they teach. The development work in EHE proved that there are better alternatives (Gray 1995).

Too difficult a solution

On the whole education does not change very much nor very easily. The reason is a general lack of agreement within the population at large as to what education is about (let alone for). We can see this at the school level where the government wants to consolidate old ways (teaching not learning) not introduce new ways (student centred not teacher centred). A romantic traditional view of learning as social engineering seems to prevail among many so-called modern educational reformers (Gray 1997). Technology is a primary factor in bringing about change or reinforcing inertia. Usually technological change has to be of a high order to be effective and modern IT is not quite well enough developed and certainly not good enough in use to bring about incontrovertible change. However, in the last few years modern IT has almost become user-friendly enough for deep change to be possible. That means this is a critical and propitious time for universities to change and adapt, to learn new ways, to become new kinds of institution. Clearly some will not do it well but it is anyone's guess which ones will adapt successfully and which ones won't. The new IT solves the problem of access to knowledge or data but it thereby destroys the current locus of control. Lecturers can no longer control access to or manipulate the content of what students learn because there are so many other sources: Open University programmes, CD-ROMs, the Internet, email. No one needs

Re-scoping the University 13

to go to university to 'find out' any more but they do need to go somewhere to know why and how. Learning (knowledge, understanding facts) is a personal matter socially embedded (Laurillard 1993). Consequently, universities are to be encouraged to move away from the presentation of information or ideas by lecturers (however distinguished) to interpersonal conversation among people who wish to explore knowledge or know how on the basis of need and interest.

Such a view is – of course – a simplification (indeed a gross oversimplification) but it makes the radical point that universities need to change the central modes through which they function if they are to do two things. One is to relate more appropriately to their clients and the other is to be more closely related to the local environment which sustains them. For some institutions this is of pressing importance. Universities embedded in the centre of a city have no difficulty in finding people who will come inside. But others – Lancaster, Lampeter and Aberystwyth are obvious examples – have no hinterland of any depth and this leaves them economically high and dry. They were conceived and structured as traditional universities in a sort of global universal space and this leaves them without the necessary key resource to change their behaviour. The new University of the Lakes (the proposed University of Cumbria) is conceived differently (Campbell-Savours 1995). The University of the Lakes has as its primary purpose the enhancement of skill levels in the population of Cumbria at large in order that greater economic prosperity might be achieved within the region. The University of the Lakes can only be effective if it engages in a continuing dialogue with all its potential customers. Not only will what it does be determined by customer need but evaluation will be by customer satisfaction. This puts it a long way from almost every other university. However, where changes have occurred (the University of Sunderland might be an example, or Thames Valley University), they are in line with the concept of the University of the Lakes in that they take their meaning and purpose (structure and modes of delivery) from customer need not the otiose comfort of academics.

Mission and management

To understand how universities might rediscover themselves we need to find new means of managing them. Current models are not very satisfactory and senior management is so extremely sensitive to criticism that external advice is usually unwelcome. Indeed, when it is sought, the advice from traditional management consultants is usually very bad. But enough is going on in universities for a reappraisal of purpose and form to be underway; there is a great deal of evidence in this book of such positive changes. The starting point should be a rethinking of mission (now understandably a somewhat old-fashioned term and better rethought as 'vision') that highlights the actual activity that lies at the core of university life. I suggested earlier that the idea of 'developing intellectual capital' fits this situation nicely but there will be variations. The usefulness of this term is its generic nature and its ability to be defined in the expression of subsidiary task and functions: teaching, research and consultancy, but also customers, clients, partners, associates and activities such as developing skills, promoting discoveries and understandings, supporting development and seeking new opportunities. These last phrases describe how those outside the university might work with those inside it.

There are implications here for management structures and styles. This is not the place to go deeply into such issues but it should be pointed out that there are currently no good examples of university management robust enough to provide us with transferable application. One reason for this is that universities have little in common with one another so far as their organizational values are concerned. Universities are loose collections of individuals and their core business centres around the idiosyncratic interests of individuals. This has been their strength and is the reason for the buying-in of talent consequent upon the Higher Education Funding Council's (HEFC) research assessment exercises. Universities depend on the very personal competencies of individuals because it is individuals who generate new knowledge and understanding. This is the real difference between FE and HE, though there is a great unwillingness to admit it for political reasons. It is the reason why FE approaches to institutional management are inappropriate to universities, and vice versa. But models of professionals working together do exist in the new industries such as electronics and medical research, advertising and the media.

Generic delivery

If the first change should be a reappraisal of purpose, the second change should be towards understanding how the generic activity takes place and how it might be delivered to those who can make use of it. Traditionally, intellectual capital has been delivered by transforming it into facts, data, opinions and models and passing it on to others through formal teaching and instruction. But increasingly it has come to be realized that the core mode of activity is learning (something which was always known but frequently overlooked). On the whole, UK educational institutions do not understand the nature of learning very well (though the now despised, so-called 'Progressive' educators did). Learning is what the individual does when engaged in a relationship with a university (i.e. people in a university). It is a process whereby individuals gain greater understanding of themselves in their world, and is therefore a reflective and enhancing holistic process. Individuals (as well as organizations) who learn increase their self-understanding and gain autonomy within organizational settings. There are any number of ways of achieving this and universities have begun to develop many of them without necessarily realizing what this means for the organization as a whole.

New ways of learning

These new developments in ways of learning include action learning (the Revans Centre at the University of Salford), problem-based learning (again at Salford and several others), networking (Sheffield and Lancaster), employee development schemes (East London and Nottingham), live projects (Sunderland, Teesside and many others), work placement (Manchester and nearly universal), career preparation (Sunderland and Central Lancashire), work-based consultancy (Huddersfield), entrepreneurship development (Sunderland and various Scottish universities), self-managed learning (Surrey), independent study (East London and Lancaster), a variety of approaches through Higher Education for Capability (HEC) (Leeds Metropolitan, Middlesex) as well as peer tutoring, practical work placements, interactive consultancy, joint research based on problem solving, and many more. Essentially, they are forms of learning partnership which take an adult view of the learner as someone who can take responsibility for their learning and organize it in their own best way (Cunningham 1994). All these approaches involve a combination of teaching, research and consultancy so that they represent the way forward for universities that really want to solve the dilemma of being equally involved in teaching, research and consultancy. Hence, the solution to their problem of finding a new mission is staring them in the face.

However, it is clear that a change in the way universities function is not enough. They have to find new ways of developing partnerships and collaborating with other agents. To do this they must move away from financial (and emotional) dependency on providers and sponsors. This will require long-term relationships and commitment beyond the easy stages of initiation and development. University staff may find this level of commitment to others oppressive, though some will find it congenial. Universities should be more often ready to take a lead, foster initiatives, commit resources and fund staff to economic and social projects. Doing this should be a central concern not a marginal one. Universities need to see the development of partnerships as the way they naturally work and collaboration as the essential characteristic of all their activities. To facilitate this it would be nice if the funding regimes changed but they have not significantly done so and the initiative falls to the institutions themselves. If university lecturers could be more modest and less intellectually arrogant, partnerships would be easier because 'mugging in' would be more acceptable.

What next?

The next few years will see a considerable expansion in HE but not necessarily through the universities. Many other agencies are in the business of developing intellectual capital, albeit in a more restricted way. Large international businesses have their own style of university (McDonald's, Microsoft,

British Aerospace and Unipart to name but a few). Large organizations have world-class research and development divisions. There is an increasing number of applied research organizations drawing their funds competitively from governments and business. There are some major research foundations (such as Rowntree, Nuffield, Kellog and Rand) that fill gaps the universities are unwilling or unable to fill. Some private institutions such as the Royal Societies engage in pump-priming activity and idea-generating that the universities can pick up on but which could be self-sustaining. The new Faraday Partnerships (*THES* 1997) indicate the way some of the new developments will go but they need to be sustained in ways that are consistent with the growth and development of the HE institutions. American universities are ready to fill gaps that can be financially profitable. Some overseas universities are beginning to attract UK students because they offer an alternative learning experience. Many universities are increasing their collaboration with non-HE partners because there is more flexibility as well as better funding outside the system.

All of this means that new opportunities are waiting to be seized but they will require new forms of organization. There is no guarantee that universities as we know them will be able to cope with the new expanding world of demand for intellectual capital. Watching the changes occur will be one of the most fascinating sideshows in HE in the next few years. Where will the development of intellectual capital take place in the early years of the new millennium?

Note

1. Originally under the dual sponsorship of Durham and Teesside Universities, University College Stockton is now an 'outpost' of Durham. Its original purpose was urban and regional regeneration as a basis for attracting inward investment. As the college has developed its purpose has become one of transformation, on the one hand of individual (and often unexpected) potential in the untypical students who attend, and on the other of communities, particularly through partnerships with industry, the local FE college, the local authority and schools. A special feature is the development of sporting activity (particularly water-based) for personal and economic renewal. The philosophy is based on the centrality of learning not teaching and the nature of interpersonal interactive activity not passive dependency (Hayward 1997).

References

Bess, J.L. (ed.) (1984) *College and University Organisation*. New York, New York University Press.
Bleaney, M.F. *et al.* (1992) What does a university add to its local economy? *Applied Economics*, 24, 305–11.
Campbell-Savours, D. (1995) *The Case for a University of the Lakes*. West Cumbria Development Agency.

Carboni, M., Oakey, D. and Sanger, J. (1996) *Learning for Capability: the Experience of the University of Salford*. Salford, Education Development Unit, University of Salford.
Cunningham, I. (1994) *The Wisdom of Strategic Learning*. London, McGraw-Hill.
Dearing, Sir R. (1997) *Report of the Committee of Enquiry into the Funding of Higher Education*. London, DfEE.
Ferlie, E., Pettigrew, A., Ashburner, L. and Fitzgerald, L. (1996) *The New Public Management in Action*. Oxford, Oxford University Press.
Fryer, R. (1997) *Report of the Committee on Adult Education*. London, DfEE.
Goddard, J. (1994) *Universities and Communities*. London, CVCP.
Gray, H. (1994) *Universities and Regional Development*. Sheffield, Training, Enterprise and Education Directorate (DfEE).
Gray, H. (1995) *Changing Higher Education*. Sheffield, SED/UCoSDA.
Gray, H. (1997) Instruction, teaching and the oppression of learners. *Capability*, 3 (1), 83-92.
Greater Manchester Universities (1995) *The Economic and Social Impact of Greater Manchester Universities*. Manchester, Communications Office, Manchester University.
Hayward, J.F.C. (1997) Personal communication.
Kennedy, H. (1997a) *Learning Works*. London, DfEE.
Kennedy, H. (1997b) *Report of the Commission of Enquiry into the Structure of Further Education*. London, DfEE.
Kermode, F. (1997) *Not Entitled*. London, Flamingo.
Laurillard, D. (1993) *Rethinking University Teaching*. London, Routledge.
Lockwood, D. and Davies, J. (1985) Universities: The Management Challenge, Guildford, SRHE/NFER Nelson.
McNicholl, I.H. (1997) *The Impact of Universities and Colleges on the UK Economy*. London, CVCP.
Middlehurst, R. (1993) Leading Academics. Buckingham, SRHE/Open University Press.
Newman, J.H. (1961) *On the Scope and Nature of University*. London, Everyman.
Schön, D.A. (1973) *Beyond the Stable State*. Harmondsworth, Penguin.
Senge, P.M. (1994) *The Fifth Discipline*. New York, Doubleday.
Skilbeck, M., Connell, H., Lowe, N. and Tout, K. (1994) *The Vocational Quest*. London, Routledge.
Times Higher Education Supplement (THES), 18 July, p. 3, 1997.

2

Knowledge Societies, Intellectual Capital and Economic Growth

David Robertson

Introduction

Governments throughout the world are striving to establish reliable connections between wealth creation and higher education (HE). Developed and emerging economies alike have been seduced by the prospect that the successful exploitation of a society's intellectual capital – the untapped stock of ideas and inventions which the most academically endowed possess – will deliver competitive advantage through improved productivity and economic growth.

The exploitation of intellectual capital generally takes two forms: first, an expansion of the HE system leading to improvements in the quality of labour stocks; and second, investment in academic capital – that is, the liberation of the research and innovation locked up in a nation's universities and research centres. Both improvements in the supply of high quality labour and the exploitation of innovative academic staff are seen as essential constituents of economic success.

Universities have become adept at presenting themselves in these terms. Gaps between the learning market and the labour market have begun to close, while business–HE round tables and policy forums are commonplace in most developed economies. Moreover, universities increasingly approach the market as a strategic resource, locked into knowledge production, regional development, a high-skills economy and job creation. As revenue from public sources has tightened, so universities have offered themselves as partners with corporations in the national innovation system. And as companies begin to describe themselves in terms of knowledge creation (Nonaka and Takeuchi 1995; Davenport and Prusak 1998), so universities respond by positioning themselves as part of the knowledge economy (Etzkowitz and Leydesdorff 1997).

Justifying public investment

This has been made necessary not just by changes in the economics of HE but by concerns expressed within the polity that HE needs to contribute in measurable terms to the creation of a knowledge society. The opening up of the 'information society', and the close attention now being paid to knowledge-intensive production, is seen to oblige universities, colleges and research centres to generate a suitable return on public investment by producing both greater volumes of highly-skilled labour and the innovations needed to refresh the economy. Accordingly, universities worldwide now defend their claims on public expenditure by reference to their potential for supporting economic growth and the revitalization of national economic assets. They have learned to emphasize the spillover effect of their work into commercially viable ventures, greater productivity and economic competitiveness.

Yet despite this propaganda, governments remain uncertain that the relationship between economic growth and investment in university-style human capital is as secure as they would wish. Increasingly, policy makers demand proof of benefit to justify increasing taxpayer cost. Universities are still perceived to be resource-hungry 'private clubs', sheltered by self-serving claims to academic autonomy which, while unassailable in democracies, make it difficult for policy makers to hold them to account. Meanwhile employer representatives complain that students qualify from HE as reproductions of the academics who taught them rather than as prospective employees ready for the ambiguities of the new labour market.

Therefore, governments have begun to ask awkward questions, often claiming to act as proxy for the interests of employers, parents and students themselves. How far do universities play a role in supplying the means for economic growth? Do the social returns justify current levels of public investment in HE? What *exactly* do universities contribute to social cohesion, regional development, lifelong learning or the quality of life? From time to time also, universities are arraigned on the charge that they may be becoming part of the private recreation industry, a much sought-after 'time-out' before immersion in the realities of economic life, a social placebo for the aspiring members of 'Generation X', but lacking direct impact on individual employment prospects or national economic success.

This chapter is an attempt to answer some of these charges by exploring how far HE has begun to shake off its pre-modern legacies in favour of a modern role within the knowledge society. Critics will continue to point to examples of obsolescence in universities; and policy makers will assume they have a role in challenging the sector with alternative lines of development. However, the evidence worldwide suggests that HE systems are sufficiently adaptive to be able to align themselves with economies driven by accelerated information exchange in societies increasingly shaped by the distribution of knowledge.

Steering changes to HE

Nevertheless, governments are not inclined to leave the repositioning of universities to chance. Over the past decade, HE has been the subject of review and reorganization, most recently in Britain (NCIHE 1997) and Australia (West 1997), but also in New Zealand, the USA, Canada, South Africa, France and Germany. These inquiries have drawn similar conclusions: universities are essential for national prosperity and for democracy; growing economies need as much HE as they can get; participating individuals benefit enormously from the experience and should pay their share; but there is a limit to public patience with self-regarding and socially exclusive institutions.

The reviews have mixed success in achieving their proposed transformations because opinion remains divided on the discipline to which HE should be subjected in order to secure appropriate changes. In Australia and New Zealand, the preference has been for a move towards the discipline of market competition, a solution that has hitherto distinguished the American response to changing economic conditions. In the UK and Europe, market competition is generally viewed by policy makers as an imperfect means by which objectives can be achieved. This is reflected in the outcome of the Dearing Inquiry in the UK (NCIHE 1997) which, while embracing some of the language of the market, proposes that perfection in these matters is best realized through the tighter external regulation and control of institutional conduct (see Robertson 1998a). The West Report (1997) in Australia, on the other hand, takes a rather different line: market competition should be extended so that institutional differentiation and student choice can be the vehicles by which signals from the labour market can be properly absorbed by the sector. In both reports, the differences of emphasis on the role of state and market mask the enduring problem of how best to ensure that HE contributes effectively to national competitiveness and wealth creation.

System-wide reviews also generate common criticisms of the sector. These appear to be expressed with a degree of politeness inversely proportionate to the frustration felt by policy makers, employers and fee-paying individuals. In Britain for example, the critique of HE which emerges from the Dearing Report (NCIHE 1997) is relatively muted, principally because the inquiry team was keen to leaven their proposals with some 'good news'. Universities appear to be changing modestly and in the right direction. Perhaps some further attention could be paid to additional financial efficiencies, new learning technologies, wider access, more lifelong learning and the skills of graduates, but otherwise the sector is about the right size, with the right balance of credentials, doing a useful job for the economy and society generally. In other words, the Dearing Report has not proposed too radical a departure from conventional practice to bring UK HE up to the millennium.

This conclusion will have come as a disappointment to those who believe that the UK university sector still largely defines itself by the criteria of an economy enjoying global prominence when universities were organized to prepare a small minority for élite positions. The restructuring of the national economy during the 1980s and early 1990s from manufacture to service production, and from growth in large organizations to expansion in the small enterprise sector, has been slow to impact on the perceptions of graduates and the practices of universities. Meanwhile employers have begun to chip away at the received wisdom that any graduate is better than no graduate. For small companies in particular, graduates can be an expensive liability who come accompanied by expectations of career continuity, seniority and task specificity. Universities have yet to experience public backlash from students as they realize that a university education does not lead naturally to privileged labour market placement, but with the introduction of tuition fee charges, this cannot now be long delayed.

In the USA on the other hand, where the private costs of HE have risen even faster than escalating public costs, public impatience is more vigorously expressed because it too spills over from the personal finance domain. The wealth-creating capacity of HE is under scrutiny from policy makers, employers and individuals alike. For example, the joint academic–business Wingspread Group on Higher Education reported in unambiguous terms that 'a disturbing mismatch exists between what American society needs of higher education and what it is receiving. The imperative for the 21st century is that society must hold higher education to much higher expectations or risk national decline' (Wingspread Group 1993: 1).

This report goes on to warn of 'a national disaster', of an HE system better equipped to discourage students than to educate them, so that 50 per cent of full-time enrolled students do not gain a degree within five years, and a similar number of registered doctoral students never obtain their final qualification. Alarmingly, the report notes that '56.3% of American-born, four-year college graduates are unable consistently to perform simple tasks of calculation'; the example cited involves working out the change from $3 after buying a $1.95 sandwich and a 60 cent bowl of soup (Wingspread Group 1993: 6).

To add to the concerns of American policy makers, the Commission on National Investment in Higher Education has reported recently that the steep rise in tuition costs would mean that, by 2015, over 50 per cent of students would no longer be able to afford to enter university if costs continued to rise at the same rate. The Commission also points out the consequences of labour market changes and wage returns for the workforce as a whole:

> The highest paid workers will hold their own to 2015. Those in the 50th percentile – workers right in the middle of the distribution – have lost about 14% in real wages over the 20 years; by 2015, they will be earning about 25% less than they earned in 1976. But the most striking consequence of current trends shows up in the figures for workers in the bottom 10%. If current trends continue, these workers will be earning little more than half of what they earned in 1976.
>
>   (Rand Organisation 1997: 4)

This assessment presents a bleak future for American HE: the public and private costs of HE are rising steeply; large numbers of students will be shut out of HE by rising costs over the next two decades; but without a university education, individuals will be unable to gain a high-paying job and will face wage degradation over the same period. The cumulative effect will be to close down the engine of economic growth – the supply effect of investment in HE – which has sustained post-war American affluence.

The ascendancy of human capital theory

Fifty years ago, the prospects seemed very different. It was American academic research which in the end delivered the technology which won the Second World War. Thereafter American university representatives were quick to persuade policy makers that their universities could 'win the peace' as well. The massive post-war public investment in American HE and its enormous expansion, mostly in the public sector institutions, was achieved by the ambiguously felicitous coupling of national security and economic growth. Mass HE was seen as a means of avoiding another economic depression while injecting growth into the post-war economy; and high level academic research could be turned to serving the new global security responsibilities which America had inherited in the wake of the conflict. As far as the interests of American universities were concerned, service of the military-industrial complex seemed an acceptable price to pay for well-found laboratories and a regular supply of students.

The contrast with the UK could not be clearer. A former head of the Department of Economic Affairs recently asked: 'Where did we go wrong?'. Noting the short-termism of policy making as a contributing factor in a 50-year economic decline, Eric Roll highlighted the fact that education and training, 'undoubtedly a most important influence on the economy' nevertheless had enjoyed over the post-war period 'fashionable interest only intermittently', and then mainly as an emergency response to economic crisis and unemployment (Roll 1995: 94). He identified neglect of human capital development over the long term as a principal explanation of loss of competitiveness.

Post-war UK policy makers have rarely been consistent in their treatment of education and training, nor demonstrated a timely appreciation of the loss of national economic vitality. They have largely been content to sponsor a small, socially selective segment of the education system, based around the academic school sixth form and restricted entry to HE, alongside a larger, employment-focused segment of low-level vocational training. An 'educational apartheid' of this kind has successfully buttressed the creaking class structure and quasi-feudal political culture of British society. Moreover, variations in policy on structures have converged with an intellectual infirmity about how to steer a modern education system – via government action or through the market – for the majority or for the academic élite.

This has produced the worst of all worlds in the UK: crisis-driven and poorly-judged supply-side interventions by government, minimal demand-side stimulation, and increased state control wrapped in the rhetoric of the market. Consequently, the UK has developed neither an effective range of provision for the population as a whole nor a particularly efficient system for producing a large enough body of high flyers by whose inventiveness a modern economy thrives. The UK simply has never released the intellectual capital of its citizens, arguably because of the destabilizing impact on its class structure, and therefore has stood by while other countries have taken its place in international markets.

Improving the quality of labour stocks

Other countries have approached the matter differently, and earlier. The post-1945 expansion of HE, in America as elsewhere, has been driven less by sociological concerns with social justice (although this may have featured in public propaganda), or status competition between groups. It has been informed almost entirely by 'human capital' considerations – that is, by the extent to which a functional fit could be achieved between the demands of growing economies, the supply of skilled labour and prospects for wealth creation.

Investment in human capital has become the most familiar argument used to support the readiness of governments to commit public expenditure on education and training. An improvement in the quantity of high-quality labour stocks has been acclaimed as the factor as important to economic growth and wealth creation as the renewal of plant and machinery (Becker 1964). Moreover (and critics would argue, significantly) investment in human capital has been explained in terms which have legitimated the transfer of investment costs from society to the individual, since the private wage returns to high skill development, at 11–20 per cent by subject, more than compensate for the private costs of entry to HE.

Although not every developed economy has pursued the switch to private investment as vigorously as the USA, every developed economy has massively expanded its stock of highly educated labour in the post-war period. In the USA itself, the shift of investment costs to the individual has not to date slowed the inclination of individuals to seek higher credentials as a means of gaining access to personal wealth-creating employment. In 1950, 2.4 million Americans attended HE programmes; by 1965 this had risen to 4.7 million; by 1980 to over 8 million; and by 1996, 14.6 million Americans were enrolled in universities and colleges.

The pattern is repeated elsewhere. In France, numbers have grown from 25,000 in 1930 to 600,000 in 1968 and over 2 million in 1997. Expansion in the UK has risen, initially more slowly, from fewer than 30,000 students in 1930 to 100,000 by 1960, and by 1997 to 1.6 million. Similar expansion gradients apply in Germany, Japan, Australia and Canada. Accordingly, the stock of graduates in the labour force now amounts to about 30 per cent or so in most industrialized countries, including the UK where the slightly lower rates of initial participation are offset by higher levels of graduate retention and achievement.

Critics of human capital theory observe that a mechanistic association of learning development with labour market productivity and personal rates of return limits the extent to which access to HE can be driven by social justice objectives. The argument runs that if one seeks an optimal 'fit' between the supply of graduates and demand for graduate skills, then access to prestigious credentials can be distorted by variations in the employment cycle, and by historic rather than prospective assessments of labour market need. Thus, policy makers will be encouraged to think in terms of functional allocations of graduate labour supply, imposing *numerus clausus* and trying to second-guess the market. They will be drawn to judgements of 'overeducation' and 'underemployment' as criteria for determining the distribution of public expenditure rather than to assessments based on socially fair access to higher learning.

While there is some strength in these arguments, and the consequences need to be addressed by public policy, human capital theory remains the most effective legitimation of the generalized expansion of HE and has served the interests of universities magnificently. Human capital theory does not prevent policy makers from engaging in labour force planning if that is their preference. It does however make a case against this approach, since the theory argues that the exchange of information from the labour market to the student (as consumer) and to the university (as producer) provides adequate signals over the long term to yield some kind of durable equilibrium. Even if a precise 'fit' cannot be achieved in terms of subject balance (all areas of the curriculum, except theology, have expanded in line with the increase in participation), the growth experienced by industrialized economies since 1945 has successfully absorbed the rising supply of graduate labour in a virtuous circle of reciprocal advantage (see Windolf 1997 for comparisons and explanations). In short, whatever policy makers may say, employers remain keen to pay for a rising supply of graduates by employing them in ever-greater numbers.

Research and the exploitation of academic capital

Human capital theory has also had a profound effect on public and private investment in research. The intensification of global competition since the 1980s has put the question of whether a conventionally structured, academically-focused, research-intensive HE can be afforded as a substantial element of public expenditure. Furthermore, universities have begun to face competition in the research market-place – from private-sector institutes, consultancies and commercial laboratories. Some of these have been direct spin-offs from universities themselves.

Table 2.1 Percentage spending on research and development

Funded by...	Companies		Government		National sources		Abroad	
	1981	1993	1981	1993	1981	1993	1981	1993
Japan	67.7	73.4	24.9	19.6	7.3	7.0	0.1	0.1
North America	48.4	57.6	49.3	39.6	2.0	2.3	–	–
EU	48.7	53.2	46.7	39.7	1.1	1.4	3.5	5.7
OECD	51.2	58.8	45.0	36.2	2.4	2.9	–	–

Performed by...	Companies		Government		HE		Private non-profit	
	1981	1993	1981	1993	1981	1993	1981	1993
Japan	66.0	71.1	12.0	10.0	17.6	14.0	4.5	4.9
North America	69.3	70.3	12.6	10.8	15.1	15.7	3.0	3.2
EU	62.4	62.6	18.9	16.5	17.4	19.5	1.4	1.4
OECD	65.8	67.4	15.0	12.7	16.6	17.1	2.6	2.9

Source: *The Economist* (1997) citing OECD sources.

These developments do not appear to have deterred governments from continuing to look to universities as a principal source of new wealth-creating research. As Table 2.1 indicates, while private companies undertake the bulk of research, governments fund substantial amounts of research and development (R&D), especially in universities. The public research funds flowing to universities show a slight decline over time but they remain significant in all economic blocs.

During the 1980s there has been a slight shift in the balance of funding from the public to the private sphere. Whereas in 1981 government and private companies funded research in equal measure everywhere except in Japan, by 1993 the balance had tipped in favour of private companies. However, this does not appear to have disturbed the balance of research undertaken by universities which remains broadly unchanged at 14–19 per cent.

Over the long term however, the balance of funding has shifted dramatically towards the public domain. For example, in 1930, only 10 per cent of research in the USA was funded by the government; by 1990, this had risen to over 60 per cent. This change can be explained largely by the growth in research funding for defence projects, although government remains the principal supplier of funds for environmental and agricultural research. Overall, the US government spent $150 billion (£95 billion) on university-based research in 1995, while the UK government contributed £4.5 billion ($7 billion) from all sources. However the funds are being distributed with increasing selectivity. For example in the USA, of the $150 billion spent by government on research, over $120 billion is spent in 100 out of nearly 4000 HE institutions (*Chronicle of Higher Education* 1997); a similar concentration of research funds has been recommended for the UK (NCIHE 1997).

The rise of academic capitalism

One noticeable impact of the shift of funding to the private sector during the 1980s has been the rise of 'academic capitalism' and the development of the entrepreneurial university. Slaughter and Leslie (1997) make the important point that 'academic capitalism' best describes what is going on because it captures both the commercialization of the research relationship and the shift of power enshrined in the change since 'fields close to the market gain power and influence within the university' (Slaughter and Leslie 1997: 218). They explain, in terms which support the direction of this discussion, that: 'Universities are the repositories of much of the most scarce and valuable human capital that nations possess, capital that is valuable because it is essential for the development of the high technology and technoscience necessary for competing successfully in the global economy' (pp. 10–11).

This academic capital is embodied in academic staff, and the search for scarce research funds has forced academics to sell their capital on the market. The private sector remains keen to purchase the outputs of academic research because of two advantages: first, universities contain publicly-subsidized academic researchers, so private costs are absorbed at the public expense; and second, universities are better placed to take on the risks of intensely original research which would otherwise impose costs on businesses if they had to anticipate the burden of failure. The problem of managing risk in research is highlighted by the experiences of companies spun-off from universities in areas such as biotechnology: initial research can yield substantial wealth to successful entrepreneurs if things go well, but massive costs also if the research stalls or fails to satisfy clinical trials.

The relationship between universities and business works the other way too. Academic entrepreneurs can intervene and add value to businesses. Research among over 400 companies identified as the fastest growing in the USA over the past five years reports major gains to growing companies from university partnerships. Growth companies that use university resources demonstrate productivity rates 59 per cent higher than peers without such relationships, and also have 21 per cent higher annual revenues and 23 per cent more capital investments. Companies which become involved with research universities in particular earn substantial benefits in increased productivity, profitability, and innovation (Coopers & Lybrand 1995).

Growth companies are also more likely to expand their university relationships beyond training and recruitment. Thirty per cent of growth companies with university ties are involved in cooperative research and development, 20 per cent use university laboratories or equipment, and 5 per cent license technologies developed in university laboratories. Furthermore, 44 per cent of companies use researchers and academic staff as technical resources, 17 per cent for business assistance and 13 per cent for manufacturing technology. Academic capitalists can provide scarce expertise and third-party objectivity in evaluating opportunities and assessing future objectives.

The emergence of the knowledge society

The changing relationship between HE and business, and the emergence of 'academic capitalism' is best explained by the development of new forms of production and demand for new kinds of labour. The fragmentation of work careers, the internal segmentation of labour markets, changes in the technology of production and the ascendancy of 'knowledge-based' production have begun to challenge the familiar university-labour market relationship. Although new jobs are predicted in those sectors of the economy well suited to the employment of graduates – the professionalized services and 'knowledge occupations' – many others are being created by small enterprises with no history of graduate employment.

The jobs that are emerging tend to emphasize functional adaptability: flexible specialization defines the 'second industrial divide' (Piore and Sabel 1984). Employers are keen to extract the maximum value not just from the labour power of employees but from their intellectual capital as well (Winslow and Bramer 1994; Stewart 1997). It is widely accepted that a nation's human resource is the one asset which competitors cannot exploit but which a successful economy must if it is to prosper. The same holds true at the level of the firm. Knowledge has become the sought-after ingredient which businesses believe will enable the successful to thrive, while the unprepared will perish (Nonaka and Takeuchi 1995). Neither large nor small companies expect to employ people by choice who lack a propensity for innovation and the successful manipulation of information. Increasingly, employers seek individuals who are capable of managing ambiguity and contradiction, who can interpret non-linear information, and who are self-organizing (Davenport and Prusak 1998).

This line of reasoning is part of a well-established tradition in social science, from Marx and Weber to Mannheim and the post-war work of Merton, Bell, Touraine, Giddens and Foucault. This tradition has charted the rise of information-as-power, the increasing influence of knowledge production on the transfer from industrial to post-industrial society, and from Fordist to post-Fordist production, the ascendancy of techno-rational production and the 'scientific estate' (Bell 1973), and the emergence of the 'information economy' (Carnoy 1993). For others, the constitution of 'information-as-product' announces the transition from modern to post-modern conditions in which knowledge becomes a commodity with an exchange value (as distinct from a use value) and can be bought and sold (Lyotard 1984: 4).

Knowledge workers come to embody a society in which institutions of government, production and education entwine (Etzkowitz and Leydesdorff 1997 refer to this as the 'triple helix'). The manufacture of meanings replaces the manufacture of things in a world dominated by 'symbolic analysts' (Reich 1991). Knowledge has been defined as 'the capacity for social action' (Stehr 1994: 95), invoking its transformational characteristics. For social historians, the dawning of the 'age of experts' and the rise of professional society is the triumph of human capital accumulation over physically embodied capital (Perkin 1989; Brint 1994). Even pessimists of this process refer to the 'rising value of the human being' as economic growth is tied to the market's 'restless search for novelty' (Lane 1991: 20).

For economists, the economic role of knowledge and information has been long understood, and not just for informing the transactions of the market-place (for example, Boulding 1966; Arrow 1984). In one influential assessment of the distribution of knowledge and human capital, Machlup (1984) defines 'knowledge work' as the characteristic of over 40 per cent of the labour force in the USA compared with 10 per cent in 1900. This may be an over-excited and methodologically dubious figure, given the occupational categories which have been bundled together under 'knowledge work', but it serves to illustrate the scale of the change from economies based on industrial and agrarian work.

In this enduring legacy of interest in the importance of knowledge to economic activity, the role of the university, knowledge production and intellectual capital remains central to the narrative. This point is reinforced by Manuel Castells in his monumental trilogy on the emergence of the 'network society'. For Castells, knowledge production, distribution and management are driving the information revolution in the same way that ownership and control of new energy sources determined the socio-political outcomes of the industrial revolution (Castells 1996). The immediate outcomes are likely to be a 'crisis of identity' among individuals, communities and nation-states; the creation of the 'powerless state' and the powerful global corporation; and the reconstruction of democracy as information becomes concentrated in the hands of those who have access to its distribution channels (Castells 1997). The lasting consequence, Castells argues, will be the rise of the 'Fourth World' – 'informational capitalism' – and massive global polarization between the information-rich nations and the rest. The rise of a global criminal economy, and apocalyptic movements of the excluded (e.g. religious fundamentalism and other forms of 'anti-knowledge' manifestations) are likely to be the social fallout from the explosion of information and its impact on global wealth creation (Castells 1998).

The properties of knowledge

What, then, are the properties of knowledge which give it such potency? What characteristics enable it to contribute so successfully to prosperity and wealth creation? The answer lies principally in its economics.

To begin with, knowledge is largely a public good. It is non-rivalrous – that is, one person's consumption does not generally diminish the ability of another to make use of the knowledge. Second, it is usually non-excludable – for example, once research findings are in the public domain, people cannot easily be excluded from drawing on them. Third, unlike labour and capital which can substitute for each other, nothing can substitute for knowledge except more knowledge. So knowledge encourages its own accumulation and renewal. Fourth, there is always an amount of personal knowledge locked up within individuals which cannot be readily extracted and mechanized. To that extent, knowledge is autonomous and cannot be 'owned'. Finally, the influence of knowledge does not diminish: it possesses an inexhaustible capacity for growth.

There may be some limitations to these conditions – some knowledge remains sensitive and classified, and other knowledge can be commercially captured (the formula for Coca-Cola, for example). Otherwise it is fair to say that the principal knowledge producers such as universities improve the stock of publicly available and economically exploitable ideas, and can do so indefinitely.

This is particularly important for economic growth. The generation of returns from human capital is the one way in which economies can modernize and refresh themselves. 'Smart' people generate 'smart' ideas, and the exploitation of new ideas is the one sure means by which mature economies can continue to grow. As new growth theorists, Barro and Sala-i-Martin explain: 'If there is no tendency for the economy to run out of ideas, then the growth rate can remain positive in the long-run' (1995: 12). Moreover, because the returns to investment in human capital do not diminish, investment is largely risk-free: the costs can always be recovered. Private rates of return to education remain broadly positive at all levels of achievement and across all societies, although returns to lower levels of education may be higher in developing economies (Schultz 1971; Psacharopoulos 1984). Generally, the risks are borne by those who do not invest in human capital accumulation. The only exceptions to this rule appear to be self-starting entrepreneurs, self-sufficient farmers, and the rich-by-inheritance.

The inexhaustible growth of ideas

The recurrent generation of bright ideas has therefore become the elixir of new economic growth (for a lucid assessment of the 'new growth theory', see Gemmell 1997). A society which arranges itself competently *both* in the creation of new ideas *and* in their productive exploitation is a society which can renew itself and prosper. While this has spawned a certain uncritical approach to the 'knowledge economy' and the 'smart company', there is little doubt that the capacity of intellectual capital to inject value into otherwise pedestrian products and processes cannot be overstated (Zuboff 1988; Stewart 1997).

Knowledge-based work becomes a struggle for perpetual self-renewal. The intensity of knowledge production and the acceleration of information exchange means that individuals, firms and societies are in a race with competitors to ensure that the latest and the newest ways of doing things are in their possession. Kay (1993: 330) re-emphasizes this point in his analysis of the foundations of corporate success:

> Historically patterns of industrial activity were heavily influenced by access to scarce natural resources ... Today these natural resource industries are much less significant ... and many of the world's most successful economies are poorly endowed with natural resources ... The scarce factors that influence national competitive advantage today are more often the range and variety of skills to be found in the workplace.

This imposes enormous responsibilities on knowledge workers for information screening and sifting, which in turn obliges them to be well-prepared in the skills required for efficient information management. Ideally, this is a function which HE should be able to discharge for people.

Latterly, the scale of this problem has become apparent to UK policy makers. Governments either side of the 1997 political watershed seem at last to have realized that economic prosperity, delivered through sustained economic growth, is no longer likely to be achieved by the conventional extraction of value from physical resources or labour power alone.

Attention over the past decade has focused on the successes of the newly industrialized economies of South East Asia which, although enjoying a relatively limited natural endowment, have generated economic growth rates for the past decade substantially in excess of most Western economies (Ashton and Green 1996). While some attempts have been made to explain these successes in terms of the social composition of Asian societies, specifically in the greater density of 'social capital' in 'high trust' societies (Fukuyama 1995), other explanations have emphasized the importance attached by these economies to the development of intellectual capital and commercially exploitable ideas through massive investment in HE. For example, Malaysia intends to become a net exporter of HE by 2020, while China plans to be producing nearly 10 million graduate scientists and engineers by the same date.

Targets of this kind assume that the Asian economies will be able to sustain the accelerated trajectories of development which have marked their progress since the early 1980s. Whether this will be possible or not depends on the sustainability of growth and trade in the increasingly interdependent global economy; on the ability of Asian economies to maintain their relative growth advantage over developed economies as their own economies mature; and on stability in the politico-economic infrastructures of these newly industrialized economies.

Universities and the 'spillover effect'

The apparent success to date of the newly industrialized Asian economies illustrates how the exploitation of 'ideas' lies at the heart of new growth theory, in particular the capacity of a society *endogenously* to generate economic growth via the extraction of value from intellectual capital. This has substantial consequences, not just for national wealth creation, but also for regional economic development.

One obvious example is the interaction of Stanford University and CalTech with the growth of Silicon Valley. Many of the initial 'start-up' companies in the emergent microcomputing industry began life as projects by Stanford researchers; for example, the joint founders of Hewlett-Packard were Stanford graduates. The transfer of the outcomes of intellectual capital from 'ideas' to commercial products was, and continues to be, iterative throughout Silicon Valley to the extent that the results of academic research are meshed seamlessly with venture capital in the pursuit of commercial viability.

Something similar exists in Massachusetts with Massachusetts Institute of Technology (MIT). Researchers at MIT regard the transfer of academic ideas from the university to the business environment as a natural feature of their professional lives. Indeed, MIT has been so successful in generating economic growth that if its commercially successful academic staff were reconstituted as a nation, they would outperform South Africa in terms of productive income. Over the years, firms spawned by MIT graduates – and these include Gillette, Digital and Campbell's Soups – now generate $230 billion and employ 1.2 million people. Fifty per cent of the firms were established by alumni within 15 years, and 15 per cent within six years of graduation.

The brains of Boston: forming the knowledge community

Rosabeth Moss Kanter has described the consequence of the spillover effect as 'the brains of Boston' in which a city of 650,000 people has become an interwoven 'knowledge community' (Kanter 1995: 201). This is a reasonable description of a city in which HE and local industry mingle seamlessly in knowledge work and wealth creation. Few cities the size of Boston contain institutions of the stature of Harvard and MIT, but this is not the whole story. In Boston alone, there are 65 universities and colleges with a student population of 250,000. Fifty per cent of the city's population attends college, many of them on a lifelong learning basis. Students make up 15 per cent of the total population of the Greater Boston area; while 35 per cent of merit scholars in the USA attend universities in Boston. In addition, there are 35 hospitals and three national medical schools. Almost 50 per cent of Boston's land area is tax-exempt and charitable property – universities, hospitals, research institutes and so forth.

Across the state as a whole, but largely because of Boston's contribution, 2.5 per cent of the US population which lives in Massachusetts gets 10 per cent of federal research funding, 10 per cent of energy research grants and 14 per cent of federal defence research grants. The impact is also felt in Silicon Valley where over 400 companies are start-ups led by graduates from MIT alone.

One line of analysis which may be worth exploring for the future is the extent to which the concentration of knowledge-intensive activities within a region generates its own economic energy. Evidence from Silicon Valley does suggest that the cross-fertilization of companies with new ideas occurs as individuals switch employers. This produces variation in the 'genetic mix' of the local economy leading to the generation of new products and new start-up companies. Under the right conditions, universities might be able to act as the 'pollinating agents' of regional economies in the future.

Conclusions: some limitations to the success story

Finally, what implications for policy can be gained from this discussion? To begin with: every university cannot be Harvard, MIT or Stanford. Most countries develop élite institutional segments which attract the bulk of the research money. This is evident in the USA with the prestigious private universities, the Ivy League and a number of public sector doctoral institutions. In Australia, the post-war emergence of the University of New South Wales and the Australian National University has complemented the extant élite segment of the big city universities. Similar patterns are observed in other major industrial societies. In the UK of course, the big ancient and civic universities have been joined by recently-established members of the research élite: Warwick, Bath, Sussex and some other institutions little more than 30 years old. In systems of HE which emphasize diversity, it is possible for knowledge-intensive, research-based and entrepreneurial institutions to emerge and prosper.

Furthermore, there is some evidence in the UK that regional knowledge economies are beginning to flourish. First, the 'spillover effect' of business development can be observed in the Strathclyde region of Scotland, around Cambridge in England, and in areas of the inner city such as the Aston Science Park in Birmingham.

Second, the narratives of success imply that all universities are entrepreneurial, that every researcher is at heart an 'academic capitalist' and that university–business relationships involve a meeting of minds in the welcoming community of knowledge work. This would of course be an overstatement. Academics do indeed generate knowledge and are keen to explore new ideas, but they will often work within a fairly tightly-drawn circle of their expertise. Moreover, in common with other professional workers, academic workers embody high levels of 'cognitive sunk costs' – that is, they invest in particular forms of human capital accumulation which have benefited them to date, namely those most valued by the university. Efforts to persuade academic staff to invest in new and entrepreneurial ways of doing things frequently meet with resistance, not because academics are unwilling to change, but because they have already incurred costs 'sunk' into familiar ways of doing things (DiMaggio and Powell 1983). It does not become efficient or rational at a professional level for individuals to sink costs into another venture unless the pay-offs are guaranteed. Thus, those 'academic capitalists' who work close to the market are likely to be those for whom the returns are great and largely guaranteed.

Third, success stories do not tell the whole story. While the 'knowledge society' promises new lines of departure for economic growth and wealth creation, it can also produce a 'jobless future' for others (Aronowitz and DiFazio 1994, Rifkin 1995). The accumulation of human capital is unevenly distributed across society, favouring the already educated and encouraging 'educational stockpiling' – that is, the tendency of the well-educated and well-paid to monopolize further human capital development (Robertson 1998b). This may lead to a state of affairs which Christopher Lasch has described as follows:

> The talented retain many of the vices of aristocracy without its virtues ... [they] have made themselves independent not only of the crumbling industrial cities but of public services in general... In effect they have removed themselves from the common life... Their ties to an international culture of work and leisure – of business, entertainment, information, and 'information retrieval' – make many of them deeply indifferent to the prospect of national decline... a class of cosmopolitans who see themselves as 'world citizens but without accepting any of the obligations that citizenship in a polity normally implies'.
>
> (Lasch 1995: 44–7, citing Reich 1991)

This may be an unduly pessimistic assessment of the emergence of the new class of 'knowledge workers', but it is possible to imagine how Lasch's world may come into being. Advanced knowledge can be managed only by those who have been prepared for the task; new knowledge can only emerge from the latest knowledge. Access to new and advanced knowledge will depend on membership of knowledge communities, notably universities or private-sector knowledge firms, and command of the pace at which knowledge is transferred – that is, command of the complex systems of communication and information exchange. The key skill, which will distinguish between individuals within knowledge communities, will be the skill which enables the individual to sift and select the right kind of information from the relevant sources, and make the necessary connections at the right time.

Under these conditions, generalized access to knowledge communities for individuals becomes not just the best way of ensuring the optimization of the accumulation of human capital for the economy as a whole; it becomes the *only* way to ensure lasting social cohesion and to prevent societies from separating into knowledge-based hierarchies of the information-rich and the information-deprived. In the end, the test of an effective relationship between universities and wealth creation lies in the success with which societies are able to manage the fair distribution of knowledge, for this is likely to determine access to the principal socio-economic assets of the future.

References

Aronowitz, S. and DiFazio, W. (1994) *The Jobless Future: Sci-Tech and the Dogma of Work*, Minneapolis, MN, University of Minnesota Press.

Arrow, K. (1984) *The Economics of Information*. Cambridge, MA, Belknap Press.

Ashton, D. and Green, F. (1996) *Education, Training and the Global Economy*. Cheltenham, Edward Elgar.

Barro, R. and Sala-i-Martin, X. (1995) *Economic Growth*. New York, McGraw-Hill.

Becker, G. (1964) *Human Capital*. Chicago, University of Chicago Press.

Bell, D. (1973) *The Coming of Post-Industrial Society: A Venture in Social Forecasting*. New York, Basic Books.

Boulding, K. (1966) The economics of knowledge and the knowledge of economics. *American Economic Review*, 56, 1–13.

Brint, S. (1994) *In the Age of Experts*. Princeton, NJ, Princeton University Press.

Carnoy, M. (ed.) (1993) *The New Global Economy in the Information Age*. London, Macmillan.

Castells, M. (1996) *The Rise of the Network Society: The Information Age – Economy, Society and Culture*, vol. 1. Oxford, Blackwell.

Castells, M. (1997) *The Power of Identity: The Information Age – Economy, Society and Culture*, vol. 2. Oxford, Blackwell.

Castells, M. (1998) *End of Millennium: The Information Age – Economy, Society and Culture*, vol. 3. Oxford, Blackwell.

Chronicle of Higher Education (1997) Almanac Issue, XLIV (1), 29 August.

Coopers & Lybrand (USA) (1995) *Report on University-Business Joint Ventures*. Washington, Coopers & Lybrand.

Davenport, T. and Prusak, L. (1998) *Working Knowledge*. Boston, MA, Harvard Business School Press.

DiMaggio, P. and Powell, W. (1983) The iron cage revisited: institutional isomorphism and collective rationality in organisational fields, in W. Powell and P. DiMaggio (eds) (1991) *The New Institutionalism in Organisational Analysis*. Chicago, University of Chicago Press.

Etzkowitz, H. and Leydesdorff, L. (eds) (1997) *Universities and the Global Knowledge Economy*. London, Pinter.

Fukuyama, F. (1995) *Trust: The Social Virtues and the Creation of Prosperity*. London, Hamish Hamilton.

Gemmell, N. (1997) *Externalities to Higher Education: A Review of the New Growth Literature*, Report no. 8 of the National Committee of Inquiry into Higher Education. London, Crown Copyright.

Kanter, R.M. (1995) *World Class: Thriving Locally in the Global Economy*. New York, Simon & Schuster.

Kay, J. (1993) *Foundations of Corporate Success: How Business Strategies Add Value*. Oxford, Oxford University Press.

Lane, R. (1991) *The Market Experience*. Cambridge, Cambridge University Press.

Lasch, C. (1995) *The Revolt of the Elites and the Betrayal of Democracy*. New York, Norton.

Lyotard, J-F. (1984) *The Postmodern Condition: A Report on Knowledge*. Manchester, University of Manchester Press.

Machlup, F. (1984) *Knowledge: its Creation, Distribution and Economic Significance*, (vol. 3 of *The Economics of Information and Human Capital*). Princeton, NJ, Princeton University Press.

NCIHE (National Committee of Enquiry into Higher Education) (1997) *Higher Education in the Learning Society* (the Dearing Report). London, Crown Copyright.
Nonaka, I. and Takeuchi, H. (1995) *The Knowledge-Creating Company*. New York, Oxford University Press.
Perkin, H. (1989) *The Rise of Professional Society: England Since 1880*. London, Routledge.
Piore, M. and Sabel, C. (1984) *The Second Industrial Divide: Possibilities for Prosperity*, New York, Basic Books.
Psacharopoulos, G. (1984) The contribution of education to economic growth: international comparisons, in M. Blaug (ed.) (1992) *The Economic Value of Education: Studies in the Economics of Education*. Aldershot, Edward Elgar.
Rand Organisation (1997) *Breaking the Social Contract: The Fiscal Crisis in Higher Education*, the report of the Commission on National Investment in Higher Education. Santa Monica, CA, RAND.
Reich, R. (1991) *Work of Nations*. New York, Simon & Schuster.
Rifkin, J. (1995) *The End of Work*. New York, Tarcher Putnam.
Robertson, D. (1998a) Who won the war of Dearing's ear? *Higher Education Review*, 30 (2), 7–22.
Robertson, D. (1998b) The University for Industry: a flagship for demand-led training, or another doomed supply-side intervention? *Journal of Education and Work*, 11 (1), 5–22.
Roll, E. (1995) *Where Did We Go Wrong?* London, Faber & Faber.
Schultz, T. (1971) *Investment in Human Capital: The Role of Education and Research*. New York, Free Press.
Slaughter, S. and Leslie, L. (1997) *Academic Capitalism: Politics, Policies and the Entrepreneurial University*. Baltimore, MA, Johns Hopkins University Press.
Stehr, N. (1994) *Knowledge Societies*. London, Sage.
Stewart, T. (1997) *Intellectual Capital: The New Wealth of Organisations*. New York, Doubleday.
The Economist (1997) 'The knowledge factory', a survey of universities. 4–10 October.
West, R. (1997) *Learning for Life*, report of the National Committee of Inquiry. Canberra, Commonwealth of Australia.
Windolf, P. (1997) *Expansion and Structural Change: Higher Education in Germany, the United States and Japan, 1870–1990*. Boulder, CO, Westview Press.
Wingspread Group (1993) *An American Imperative: Higher Expectations of Higher Education*. Racine, WI, Johnson Foundation. Johnson Foundation Wingspread Group.
Winslow, C. and Bramer, W. (1994) *FutureWork: Putting Knowledge to Work in the Knowledge Economy*. New York, Free Press.
Zuboff, S. (1988) *In the Age of the Smart Machine*. New York, Basic Books.

3

How Universities Can Thrive Locally in a Global Economy

John Goddard

Introduction

This chapter focuses on how universities can best handle a new set of demands being placed upon them by a new set of actors and agencies, namely those concerned with regional development. What is the basis of these new demands? In the past, higher education (HE) in most countries has been primarily funded by national governments to meet national labour market needs for skilled manpower and to provide a capacity to meet national research and technological development needs. In terms of HE management this has generally meant a single paymaster, relatively secure long-term funding, the education of a readily identifiable and predictable population of full-time students in the 18–24 year age range, destined to work in the corporate sector, and the provision of a well-founded infrastructure to support the pursuit of individual academic research and scholarship. Such a regime imposes limited demands on university management and indeed supports the ethos of academic self-management and collegiality.

This model is being challenged at the national level by moves from an élite to a mass system of HE and a new emphasis on lifelong learning, by the pursuit of efficiency gains in public funding, by the rise of new modes of knowledge production and distribution outside of universities which are challenging the university monopoly and by the opportunities for new ways of delivering education and training made possible by information and communication technologies. Each of these developments challenges the privileged relationship between universities and national ministries of education as new clients for research and learning and new intermediaries articulating these demands come forward. Characteristically these new players pursue an agenda which is local or regional in character: small and medium sized enterprises (SMEs) represented by chambers of commerce; lifelong learners by community development associations and local labour market agencies; arts and cultural industries by local authorities and new media interests by globally backed local cable companies. These bodies recognize that universities have much to offer through locally relevant knowledge production; as gateways to global information resources; in human capital formation through creating a flexible, adaptable workforce; and in providing leadership within formal and informal local governance structures.

Responding to these demands clearly poses management problems for traditional universities. Many have created intermediary organizations like technology transfer and regional development offices to provide a gateway to the wider world. The challenge now is to bring this activity into the mainstream and embed regional engagement into academic life more generally. This chapter seeks to start this process by reviewing the latest thinking about regional development through notions of the learning region and its governance, and thereby deepening understanding of the forces which are raising the importance of the regional dimension for universities, industry, commerce and economic development authorities.

The learning region

There is a growing body of academic research on the role of universities in regional development. Much of this has been narrowly concerned with two issues: economic analyses of the direct employment effects associated with staff and student spending in the local economy, and technology transfer, particularly through the creation of spin-off companies and the establishment of science parks (Goddard *et al.* 1994; van der Meer 1996). More recently the role of universities in regional development has been seen as going beyond this narrow technical and economic approach to embrace the role of universities in enhancing the stock of human capital within a region. Examples include recruiting students from without the region and placing them with local companies; programmes of continuing and professional development to enhance the skills of local managers; locally embedding global businesses by targeted training programmes and research links; providing a gateway to the global knowledge base for SMEs; and last but not least, providing strategic analysis and leadership within local civil society. The fact that such opportunities for a wider role for universities are arising can be traced to fundamental shifts in the organization of production and the related regulation of the economy reflected in the twin processes of globalization and localization. For effective engagement in the regional development process it is vital that university managers have a basic understanding of these dynamics. The following section sketches in the principal themes.

Reconceptualizing regional development

The enormous transformations in the nature of the capitalist world economy since the mid-1970s have had major implications for economic development strategies and their governance. First, the stability of production systems, product markets and national corporate relations have been undermined by the rate of technological change, most notably through the widespread effects of generic or carrier technologies such as information and communication technologies (ICTs). Technological innovation and access to resources for innovation (skills, knowledge, information) have therefore become central to the competitive strategy of firms, which have developed new flexible structures to better utilize and capture such advantages on a global scale. States have recognized the need to maintain a position on the leading edge of technology if they are to maintain employment and growth, and hence there is an increasing attention to policies to support and promote research and development (R&D), innovation and technology transfer.

Notwithstanding this policy orientation, the globalization of finance and of the organization of production – underpinned by ICTs that permit the flexible reshaping and reconfiguring of investment and resources – has weakened the bargaining power of the nation state. International bodies have encouraged greater freedom in the flow of goods and information such that it is now the nature of the production locality as much as national market characteristics that determines investment decisions. Not only has regional or local intervention become more important to economic success, but there has also been a qualitative shift in the form of local policy towards indigenous entrepreneurship and innovation, and to providing a more sophisticated environment for mobile capital so as to maximize local value added (R&D and other high status jobs, successful and therefore growing firms).

The importance of this perspective for managing firms and localities has been neatly captured by Kanter in her recent book *World Class* which is significantly subtitled *Thriving Locally in the Global Economy* (Kanter 1995). According to Kanter, future success will come to those companies, large and small, that can meet global standards and tap into global networks. And it will come to those cities and regions that do the best job of linking the businesses that operate within them to the global economy. She argues that forces of globalization are so powerful that communities must connect the global and the local and create a civic culture to attract, and retain or 'embed' footloose investment. The challenge is to find ways in which the global economy can work locally by unlocking those resources which distinguish one place from another. The essential argument here is that universities can provide a vital locational asset within the global economy.

Kanter goes on to argue that in the face of these globalizing pressures, organizations have no alternative but to continually improve and attempt to be world class by paying attention to what she calls the 3 Cs: concepts, competence and connections. She links this to geography by suggesting that 'world class places can help grow these assets by offering innovative capabilities, production capabilities, quality skill, learning, networking and collaboration' (Kanter 1995: 35). The location of universities in regions is a powerful facilitator of these processes – concepts links to research;

competence links to teaching; and connections links to the transfer to and from a region of people and networks grown out of universities.

In order to realize such policy shifts, local policy has needed to be innovative and entrepreneurial itself, typically through drawing on a wider network of resources, negotiating and building alliances between local and other tiers of government, universities, private sector interests and non-profit organizations. Thus the successful entrepreneurial municipality shifts from being an arm of the national welfare state to a catalyst for local cooperation and policy innovation.

Regional success has been characterized by a range of different models, but with a common agreement as to the factors underpinning success: agglomeration economies, economies of scope, trust, networks of small firms and supportive institutions. Central to successful innovation are the structures and modes of interaction between knowledge producers, disseminators and users. Since technologies embody both people and ideas as well as physical artefacts, transactions involving extensive interaction and iterative communication are widely believed to be necessary as a means of facilitating exploitation. This 'organized' method of exchange can encompass both physical technology and/or employees – including producers, disseminators and users – moving between institutions while maintaining close linkages, for instance, between universities and linked spin-off companies.

Within this overall policy environment geographical differences in the nature of cultures, institutions and legacies of past industrial practices will clearly influence the effectiveness of the dissemination of knowledge between and within institutions whether at the national or regional level. Differences are particularly evident if interpreted as uneven capabilities in effectively organizing, through informal or formal means, market transactions. For example, Lundvall illustrates the importance of a common culture and language shared by users and producers to facilitate the transmission and translation of highly encoded information such as R&D results (Lundvall 1988). Differences in training cultures and attitudes towards technology are also crucial to the effectiveness of modes of communication and exchange.

Studies of economically successful regions suggest that their success depends on what Amin and Thrift (1994: 14) term 'institutional thickness' or what Putnam (1993: 167) calls 'social capital'. Although difficult to define, this institutional thickness is more than simply a strong presence of institutional bodies and practices supporting enterprise. The institutions should have high levels of interaction, leading to structures of domination or coalition that can achieve collective representation of interests, and a mutual awareness of a common purpose: what Amin and Thrift (1994) term a 'collectivisation and corporatisation of economic life'. An attempt to shape the governance structures in local economic development in a way that increases the likelihood of a beneficial impact must therefore be cognisant of the culture, social structures and politics of the institutional networks linking policy actors and the firms they seek to influence.

Defining the learning region

In the context of the role of universities in economic development, the most helpful approach to operationalizing these ideas can be found in the concept of the learning economy which emerges from studies of national systems of innovation (see Lundvall 1992; Lundvall and Johnson 1994). Here Lundvall stresses the importance of interactive learning as the basis for innovation and change in modern developed economies. He defines the learning economy in the following terms: it is an economy where the success of individuals, firms and regions reflects the capability to learn (and forget old practices); where change is rapid and old skills get obsolete and new skills are in demand; where learning includes the building of competencies, not just increased access to information; where learning is going on in all parts of society, not just high-tech sectors; and where net job creation is in knowledge-intensive sectors (high R&D, high proportion of the population with a university degree with the result that the job situation worsens for the unskilled).

Within the learning economy different kinds of knowledge can be identified. First, 'know what' – that is, facts and information. Second, 'know why' – that is, principles and laws necessary to reduce trial and error. Third, 'know how' – that is, the skills and capability to do something; skills that are traditionally acquired within the workplace. Fourth, 'know who' – that is, information about who knows how to do what and the social capability to establish relationships with special groups in order to draw on their expertise. Each of these different forms of knowledge uses different channels for information exchange. In the case of 'know what' and 'know why', formal learning in schools and universities is the normal channel. 'Know how' depends on practical experience through tacit learning (for example, through apprenticeships), but also increasingly through network relationships with industrial and commercial partners. Finally, 'know who' is learned from social interaction via professional associations, day-to-day dealings with customers, subcontractors and a wide range of other actors and agencies.

Network knowledge, in relation to 'know-how', is worthy of special attention, because it is a hybrid form of knowledge that is neither completely public nor completely private. It depends on trust – not the market – and is characterized by such considerations as reliability, honesty, cooperation and a sense of duty to others. Network knowledge refers not only to the skills of individuals but the transfer of knowledge from one group to another to form learning systems – the institutional infrastructure of public and private partnerships. Because network knowledge is highly dependent on interpersonal relations, it can most readily be developed within a particular region. Thus Florida (1995: 32) argues that to be effective in this increasingly borderless global economy,

> regions are increasingly defined by the same criteria and elements which comprise a knowledge-intensive firm: continuous improvement, new

ideas, knowledge creation and organisational learning. Regions must adopt the principles of knowledge creation and continuous learning; they must in effect become learning regions.

Key to such a learning region is the human infrastructure and the institutional mechanisms that foster interactive learning and a central part of this infrastructure, in terms of the reproduction and adaptation of human resources, is the university.

In the case of human capital, universities in many countries have traditionally produced raw graduates for a national labour market dominated by large employers, with little concern for SMEs or graduate retention in local labour markets. This model has begun to break down in response to changing patterns of employer demands such as the decentralization of large corporations into clusters of smaller business units and the greater role of smaller businesses as subcontractors, suppliers, franchisees etc. Such trends have important implications for the skills required of graduates and the location of the firms' recruitment decisions. It is therefore not surprising that regional agencies are promoting graduate retention initiatives as a way of upgrading the stock of higher-level local skills. In parallel with these demand-side changes the expansion of HE provision together with rising numbers experiencing the need to change career later on in life is leading to a growing supply of mature local students for undergraduate and postgraduate programmes.

Notwithstanding these developments, very little is known about the flow of students through HE into local labour markets and how this relates to the overall economic performance of regions. Yet a key characteristic of the learning region is the way in which knowledge is transferred from one group to another to create learning systems. In terms of universities this includes knowledge of the appropriate skills and competencies required of the workforce.

What constitutes 'appropriate skills' will depend on the overall regional development strategy, be it indigenous development based on local enterprise, exogenous development based on attracting inward investment, or a combination of the two, for example by upgrading local suppliers to support and 'embed' inward investment. In this context, the analogy between regions and organizations is one where the shift is from personnel management, based around handling individual employment contracts and personal development, to human resource management, which harnesses people development to the strategic objectives of the organization. So the key question becomes: 'Does the region include a human resource development as part of its overall strategy?' This question raises a number of specific challenges concerning the *type* of training programme, *what* institutions are best placed to provide the programme, and *where* within the region, or for that matter outside, this provision should occur.

Hence, an obvious requirement of a regional human resource strategy is information about future labour market needs. Given the long time-lag between the identification of needs and the development of the necessary skills, one of the fundamental requirements of a learning region is the sharing of intelligence between the education and training system and employers. In addition to ensuring that the education and training system produces people with the flexibility to respond to changing labour market circumstances, attention has to be paid to the specific skills and competencies required by particular industries and/or occupations.

Labour market intelligence focuses on the direct contribution of universities to the economic success of their localities. A further question concerns the indirect contribution of universities to the social and cultural basis of effective democratic governance and, ultimately, economic success. For example, Putnam (1993: 171) has shown the strong relationship between civic culture and institutions – understood as 'norms of reciprocity and networks of civic engagement' – and wider socio-economic performance. Regions or localities that are rich in such networks 'encourage social trust and co-operation because they reduce incentives to defect, reduce uncertainty, and provide models for future co-operation' (p. 172). In so far as universities are by tradition classically 'civic' institutions, they can play a key role in the development of the cultural and political determinants of socio-economic success. A key challenge is to enhance the role which universities, and their staff and students, play in the development of such networks of civic engagement, and hence in the wider political and cultural leadership of their localities (for example, through the formal and informal engagement of universities in local political processes, through university staff serving as elected politicians or providing a source of advice for local government, through contributions to the media, etc.).

Implications for university management

The implications of many of the processes of globalization and localization that have been outlined have yet to be addressed by most universities. Kanter (1995) refers to four aspects of globalization: simultaneity, multiple choice, pluralism and resource mobility. Simultaneity refers to the fact that we can no longer rely on spatial and temporal lags associated with the diffusion of new education products and services – universities can no longer hide behind the barriers of time and space. Multiple choice (or bypass) refers to the way in which local or territorial monopolies are broken down, such that universities can no longer rely on a local monopoly in education provision as new providers using distance learning techniques enter their patch. Pluralism is the process by which old centres of power are continually challenged such that older universities can no longer guarantee their dominant position as students and firms exert consumer choice. Finally, resources – particularly the élite or so-called 'cosmopolitans', who carry ideas around in their heads, and possess global networks of contacts – are becoming more mobile, shifting their place of residence more frequently, and this applies no less in academia than in the private sector.

In the face of these threats, universities have no option but to attempt to tie down the global within the local; in so doing they will find willing partners in the public and corporate sector where similar pressures are being confronted. As in other sectors universities will have to reappraise their governance structures and management processes in the light of this challenge, and national government will have to reconsider policies for funding and regulating HE.

The scale of the challenge should not be underestimated. Adjusting the curriculum to the rapidly changing needs of employers and the labour market provides a good example. In terms of Lundvall's (Lundvall 1992; Lundvall and Johnson 1994) description of the learning economy, while universities have been good at the 'know what' and 'know why' aspects of education, and are improving on the 'know how' aspects through incorporation of the tacit learning acquired via work placements into teaching programmes, the 'know who' dimension is altogether more problematic. Progress on this front implies a deep relationship between research and teaching based on the sharing of the network knowledge of the research endeavour with students at all levels.

When considering their relationship with industry in a regional context universities need to consider themselves as being located at the head of a supply chain which is devoted to the provision of knowledge. The distribution channels for this knowledge are through students (projects and placements), graduates and postgraduates, as well as through published and contract research and consultancy that lead to new and improved technologies and management processes. But unlike a business enterprise situated in a similar supply chain position, universities devote relatively little resources to marketing their products in the form of graduates or to responding to signals about what the market wants. They simply have a sales department, in the form of the careers service, which has no ability or mechanisms to match output (quality, quantity or specification) to customer needs.

The market-place is, of course, extremely complex because it is composed of the totality of organizations that currently, or might in the future, employ graduates. At one end of the spectrum are tightly regulated vocational markets like medicine, architecture, law and engineering. At the other end of the spectrum are the largely unarticulated demands of SMEs. If universities are to play a more active role in economic development, it is vital that they understand the market, segment it and use this information to guide their teaching activities. This means not simply responding to currently expressed wants but actively researching the dynamics underlying changing employer needs and treating students as clients and employers as the end customer.

In some countries the fact that this approach is far from universal can be partly attributed to the student funding regime which currently rewards 'production' but not 'sale'. In consequence the marketing function is often poorly developed. If universities were in part rewarded for the delivery of graduates into employment, including local employment, they would clearly have an incentive to put more effort into marketing and economic development.

However, becoming a market-led organization requires a major change in university culture. It implies a strong sense of institutional purpose, whereas universities remain dominated by academics whose principal professional loyalty is to their national or international invisible college rather than their parent institution. The 'new production of knowledge' described by Gibbons *et al.* (1994) involves partnerships with the users and beneficiaries of research that transcend institutional boundaries and which are difficult to integrate with formal institutional planning and resource allocation. According to Gibbons *et al.* new patterns of strategic alliances between academic groups based on complimentary competencies may occur, but not between institutions within a region.

In short, improved integration of universities with regional development will not be readily achieved by top-down planning mechanisms at either the institutional or regional level but by ensuring that the various stakeholders in the regional development process – education and training providers, employers and employers' organizations, trade unions, economic development and labour market agencies, and individual teachers and learners – have an understanding of each others' role and the factors encouraging or inhibiting greater regional engagement. For example, there needs to be an understanding that universities and labour market agencies work in the context of national HE policy, labour market training targets, global competitive pressures to downsize and outsource and personal financial constraints on students to invest in learning.

While national governments may seek to increase the engagement of universities with economic development, the means of achieving this goal is far from clear, particularly in the context of the value universities attach to individual autonomy. Such autonomy is associated with a diversity of institutions, often on a regional as well as a national scale – a pattern which has evolved historically. For those universities with a strong research base, regional issues may be of minor concern. Such institutions see themselves as serving the region by attracting students from outside, with those students who remain adding to the local stock of human capital. They also contribute to attracting inward investment and possibly embedding that investment through training and research links. Such institutions thus contribute to exogenous regional development. Nevertheless, even within research-based universities, certain departments, degree programmes and research activities will have strong regional linkages.

Alongside such institutions in most regions are those where serving the local and regional community remains a central component of their mission. Regional universities also have national and international links that can provide gateways to the wider world for local firms and students. Finally, between these extremes there may be universities which are trying to develop their research base in selected fields and in the process are devoting considerable resources to 'going global'. Determining which particular mix of institutions, and more importantly which mix of teaching and research programmes, would best underpin the economic development of a region is a key challenge. With the right form of incentives in terms of government procedures for university assessment and leadership development programmes, it might be possible to ensure that the appropriate signals reach and are embedded into the programmes of individual universities.

As regards assessment, regional criteria could be incorporated into national teaching and research assessment exercises. In addition, a strong case can be made for establishing a regional assessment process undertaken by universities themselves. Such assessments could be done with the aid of consultants with expertise in economic development and HE management. The assessments would cover institutional organization, teaching, research and other services actually or potentially relevant to regional needs. The outcome of the assessment could be linked to a government development fund for pump-priming initiatives which seek to enhance the university's contribution to economic development. Institutions would be free to participate in such a scheme and/or confine it to those parts of their activity that they deem to be regionally relevant.

Alongside such assessments it would be necessary to have a programme of human resource development targeting those individuals inside and outside of universities that have boundary-spanning functions relevant to joint working on economic development. One of the key factors of success in regional partnerships is the presence of 'animateurs' who act as gatekeepers between different organizations/networks. A small number of staff in universities, labour market and economic development agencies, and dynamic businesses hold positions in which extra-organizational networking is a central feature of their job. People who hold such a position will do so by virtue of their personal and professional competency; they nevertheless require developmental support for their own professional improvement, and moral support from individuals and groups around them. For the most part the necessary skills and attributes are intuitive and learned through practice; however the growing need for such people suggests that some more fundamental training and support is required. Relevant skills include: networking; facilitation; working with alternative cultures; setting up projects; planning and contract management; raising financial support; personal organization; supervision and personal support techniques; insight into organizational policies; and dynamics. The establishment of such a development programme for individuals engaged in the university/regional interface would be a further small positive step towards its improved management. Similar strictures apply to other stakeholders concerned to raise regional competitiveness.

Acknowledgements

This chapter is based on a background paper for a project on 'The response of higher education institutions to regional needs' being led by the author on behalf of the Organization for Economic Cooperation and Development (OECD) programme on Institutional Management in Higher Education. The chapter draws on a report prepared for the UK Department for Education and Employment (1998) on *Universities and Regional Development* by a group of researchers and managers at the University of Newcastle working through its Newcastle School of Management (chief executive, Dr Roger Vaughan). Other members of the team were Dr Madeleine Atkins, dean of the faculty of education; Dr Roger Vaughan; Dr Richard Firth, director of the careers service; Richard Tomlin, director of research services; and John Dersley, university regional development officer. I would also like to acknowledge the contributions of my colleague from the Centre for Urban and Regional Development Studies, Dr David Charles.

References

Amin, A. and Thrift, N. (eds) (1994) *Globalisation, Institutions and Regional Development in Europe*. Oxford, Oxford University Press.
Department for Education and Employment (1998) *Universities and Regional Development*. Newcastle, Newcastle School of Management.
Florida, R. (1995) Toward the learning region. *Futures*, 27(5), 527–36.
Gibbons, M., Limoges, C., Nowotny, H., Schwartzman, S., Scott, P. and Trow, M. (1994) *The New Production of Knowledge*. London, Sage.
Goddard, J.B., Charles, D.R., Pike, A., Potts, G. and Bradley, D. (1994) *Universities and Communities*. London, Committee of Vice Chancellors and Principals.
Kanter, R.M. (1995) *World Class: Thriving Locally in the Global Economy*. New York, Simon & Schuster.
Lundvall, B-Å. (1988) Innovation as an interactive process: from user-producer interaction to the national systems of innovation, in G. Dosi *et al.*, *Technical Change and Economic Theory*. London, Frances Pinter.
Lundvall, B-Å. (ed.) (1992) *National Systems of Innovation. Towards a Theory of Innovation and Interactive Learning*. London, Frances Pinter.
Lundvall, B-Å. and Johnson, B. (1994) The learning economy. *Journal of Industry Studies*, 2, 23–42.
Putnam, R.D., with Leonardi, R. and Nanetti, R.Y. (1993) *Making Democracy Work: Civic Traditions in Modern Italy*. Princeton, NJ, Princeton University Press.
van der Meer, E. (1996) *Knowledge on the Move: The University as a Local Source of Expertise*. Amsterdam, University of Amsterdam.

4

Measuring the Economic Impact of Universities: Canada

Fernand Martin and Marc Trudeau

Introduction

In competing for scarce government funds, many sectors – from theatre-arts groups, to stadiums for sports franchises, to whole industries – have tried to justify public support by conducting studies that show the economic gains from a public investment. The university sector is no exception – many studies conducted by individual universities have quantified the regional economic benefits, in terms of increased spending and jobs, of their research and educational functions.

The traditional input-output (I-O) impact studies used to calculate economic benefits have been similar for all sectors, but it has become apparent that these methods have shortcomings. In particular is the failure of Canadian economic impact studies that use Statistics Canada's I-O models to take into account the cost of not choosing an alternative (and perhaps more beneficial) investment or to distinguish between the differing nature of the activities. For example, it would be inappropriate to presume that the economic impacts of subsidizing a sports franchise would be comparable to those from providing funding for a university – yet that is what a standard I-O analysis will show. This type of distinction is especially important in assessing the economic impact of activities such as university research that not only spend money but affect the productivity of the overall economy. In effect, universities have two distinct, measurable contributions to the economy, only one of which is measurable using standard economic impact models.

The first, 'static' effect is similar to other economic activities: they spend money. Numerous universities in Canada have used standard I-O models to measure the gross domestic product (GDP) and employment contribution to their local economies. Quantifying these economic benefits has become even more important in recent years because of reduced government funding and the fact that many smaller universities have regional economic development as an integral part of their mandate. While these studies serve their purpose, there is an increasing recognition among university administrators and economists alike that the primary benefits from universities, especially university research, come not from the fact that they spend money but from the knowledge they generate and transmit. In failing fully to take into account this 'dynamic' effect, traditional I-O models tend to underestimate the true impact of university research.

The 'dynamic' impact of universities and their research work is not only more important but is absent in most other industries. It differentiates universities from virtually all other economic activity because universities generate and disseminate knowledge and technology which in turn increase the productivity of factors of production, thereby increasing GDP. Though the benefits of university research and scholarly activities are well known, they have been, and remain, difficult to quantify. Some of the recent university economic impact studies have attempted to quantify these dynamic effects.

For example, work done at the University of Calgary estimated the economic benefits of the University by putting dollar values on its research by estimating the value of faculty consulting activities and the impact of research on public policy. Another notable example is the study conducted for the Université de Montréal which theorized that knowledge-intensive industries would not be able to prosper in Montreal without university research. The presence of these industries is in part a direct consequence of the presence of high quality, research-intensive universities, and this economic impact can be measured. Conducting a similar study on a national scale uses many of the same assumptions but requires a different methodology.

This chapter combines the dynamic and static impacts of Canadian university research in the age of the competitive global knowledge economy. The first section will use the Statistics Canada I-O model to provide an estimate of the static impact of university research in order to allow comparison with other economic impact studies. This is where it will be shown that gross I-O analysis usually overestimates the net static impact on the economy. The second, theoretical section will provide an overview of the current growth literature, emphasizing the role of universities in producing the intellectual capital that drives innovation and economic growth. The third section will operationalize the second section by providing a quantitative estimate of the impact of university research on the Canadian economy. This section uses the previously outlined growth theory to develop models that permit an accurate calculation of the dynamic impact.

Measuring the static economic impact of university research

This section quantifies the static economic benefits of the $4.3 billion university research enterprise and estimated $543 million in graduate student expenses. University research, like any other expenditure, results in extra money being spent in other sectors of the economy. The static impact is

Table 4.1 Gross static economic impact of R&D university expenditures (year 1994/5)

	GDP at factor cost (billion $)	Jobs
University R&D expenditures (direct-indirect-induced)	4.657	73390
Student subsistence expenditures	0.309	8032
Total	4.966	81422

essentially the measurement of the effect of this extra spending on the rest of the economy.

The gross static impact

The gross static economic impact is the calculation, using the Statistics Canada Open I-O Model, of the impact of the research and development (R&D) activities of Canadian universities.[1] The Statistics Canada I-O Model permits an accurate calculation of the value of this economic activity as it works its way throughout the economy. For example, the money spent by universities on research will directly support the staff employed at universities as well as the companies that supply the universities with the goods and services (such as laboratory equipment, electricity and office supplies) required to conduct research – this is the direct impact. The indirect impact arises from the money spent on goods and services by the direct suppliers. The sum of the incomes earned by the employees of universities and their suppliers, net of deductions for taxes and savings, is called the induced effect. In summary, the cycle of economic activity resulting from university expenditure takes the form of:

- purchases of goods and services with salaries and wages paid to university employees;
- purchases by suppliers of goods and services used in research activities;
- graduate student expenditures on basic consumption goods and services; and
- the expenditure by the universities' employees and those of their suppliers.

The value of this economic activity is calculated using the multiplier from the Statistics Canada I-O Model. The results of the direct, indirect and induced effects, in terms of GDP and jobs, are provided in Table 4.1.[2]

The results of the gross static impact suggest that the university research enterprise is responsible for almost $5 billion of Canada's GDP and over 81,000 jobs. This represents almost 1 per cent of Canadian GDP and over 0.5 per cent of the Canadian workforce. These results are impressive and compare favourably with studies done in other countries, such as the UK, particularly since our study takes into account only university research while others typically measure the impacts of all university expenditures.[3] As mentioned previously, we go beyond the standard impact study such that the next section will correct for some imperfections in the standard methodology.

Net economic impact

The I-O model used by Statistics Canada is a reasonably accurate simulation of the Canadian economy, but some of its working hypotheses are not completely representative of the actual economy. For example, the model cannot incorporate resource constraints or price changes that can arise from economic activity. Consequently, the gross impact results presented in Table 4.1 must be adjusted to account for the constraints imposed by the model. This involves three adjustments which, when made, will provide a more accurate measurement of the true economic impact of university research. First, some of the expenditures included in the calculations of the gross impact would have been made whether university research existed or not. Second, the Statistics Canada I-O Model overestimates the results because it does not take into account the effect on government finances of public investment in university research.[4] Third, the impact arising from the induced effects is overstated because the Statistics Canada I-O Model is not completely closed and should be eliminated.

On the expenditure side – adjustments one and two – the economic impact is overstated and should be adjusted to account for the following negative effects:

- subsistence expenditures of Canadian graduate students would occur whether these individuals are in university or not;
- GDP would increase had graduate students held jobs rather than pursue further study, earning income that would partly be consumed and producing goods and services;
- government subsidies for university R&D must be financed from taxes, government debt or the reduction of other government expenditures; and
- induced effects.

In terms of GDP and jobs, the overestimation resulting from these negative impacts can be found in Table 4.2. The adjustments signify that the gross static impact should be adjusted downwards by $3.456 billion and 67,845 jobs.

It follows that the net static economic impact of university research is the difference between its gross static impact and the adjustments listed in Table 4.2. The results, provided in Table 4.3, signify that the net static impact of university research is $1.507 billion in GDP and 13,577 jobs. This is less than one-third of the gross static impact, representing only about one-third of 1 per cent of GDP and less than one-tenth of 1 per cent of the

Table 4.2 Overestimation of GDP by the gross static economic impact of R&D university expenditures

Cause of overestimation for 1994/5	GDP at factor cost (billion $)	Jobs
Induced effect	1.346	19904
Student expenditures	0.225	5849
Loss of student supplementary production	0.653	14152
Government subsidies	1.235	27940
Total overestimation	3.456	67845

Table 4.3 The net static economic impact of R&D university expenditures

1994/5[5]	GDP at factor cost (billion $)	Jobs
Net GDP	1.507	
Net jobs sustained		13577

labour force. While these results may seem insignificant, simply having a positive net static economic impact is a sign that university research has a more significant economic impact than other sectors of the economy. It must also be remembered that the real benefits of university research come not from its spending power, but from the increases in GDP arising from better trained graduates and more efficient, more productive companies. It is to measuring this impact that we now turn.

The dynamic impact of university research

Innovative firms and individuals are widely seen to be crucial elements in ensuring a wealthy economy. Recent research into innovation and economic growth has resulted in a new terminology that can shed light on the important role of university research. Recent research also suggests that three durable factors of production lead to sustained economic growth: hardware, software and wetware.[6] Hardware includes the traditional physical capital goods and infrastructure such as roads, airports, natural resources and plant, machinery and equipment. Software consists of knowledge, technology and information that can be reused, stored, copied and communicated using various technologies such as computer disk, film, blueprint, etc. Wetware, on the other hand, is composed of all knowledge and information 'stored in the "wet" computer of the brain'[7] and includes the traditional notion of human capital found in the new economic growth theories.

One can easily see the importance of universities in this nomenclature given that universities not only produce software, but provide individuals with the wetware necessary to function in the knowledge-based economy. Both software and wetware are then used to make hardware more productive, producing a further increase in GDP.[8] Universities are also crucial for innovation because they not only produce software and wetware but aid innovation by diffusing that knowledge to various sectors of the economy. The following sections present a theory and methodology that will enable a reasonably accurate measure of the dynamic impact of university research.

Universities and innovation

There are a number of popular examples of university research fostering innovation which has become the foundation on which is built a vibrant, growing, knowledge-intensive economy. Examples include the corridor of high technology companies in Boston extending down Route 128 from Massachusetts Institute of Technology (MIT) (among others), and the computer industry in Silicon Valley near Stanford University. However, less well known are world-class Canadian growth poles, such as the concentration of biotechnology and agri-food companies around the University of Saskatchewan in Saskatoon, the numerous environmental science and medical companies connected with McMaster University in Hamilton or the many patent drug companies in Montreal linked with McGill University and Université de Montréal. Clearly, the proximity of these technology clusters to high quality, research-intensive universities illustrates the impact that universities can have on area economies.

Innovation is fostered when wetware and software are diffused to skilled and knowledgeable personnel in the university and private sectors who have the prescience to see unrelated applications. It is this interaction, the ability of these people to see connections where none existed before, that makes concentrations of learned personnel so desirable. Universities become valuable to the economy because they provide the high-quality personnel, as well as much of the knowledge and technology, required by innovative firms. As the Organization for Economic Cooperation and Development (OECD) *Oslo Manual* (1996b) states: 'many areas of basic research provide fertile ground for the training of skilled technology-oriented scientists – whose experience can often be successfully directed to industrial problems'.[9] Universities create knowledge and increase productivity by supplying human capital (graduates), conducting their own research (basic or applied), and through the consulting activities of their faculty. Of course, universities are not the only location consideration for firms but they can be a necessary condition. They permit certain regions to attract, retain and generate high-technology industries.

Not only do university researchers work in cooperation with industry, but frequently university research produces knowledge or processes that are spun-off from their institutions or have the rights sold to private sector companies who then develop the technology.[10] University technology transfer offices are very active across Canada in transferring knowledge for commercial application, creating leading-edge companies, high-quality jobs and economic growth.[11] University expertise is also important for non-technology, social and organizational innovation. Professor-consultants play a significant role in the system of innovation as they provide knowledge and advice to Canadian firms. Scientific knowledge comprises not only products and processes but also organizational methods and knowledge embodied in people either by formal training or by learning by doing. The important realization here is that university researchers foster innovation of all kinds as a result of their experience doing so-called basic research.

Innovation is a process dependent on individuals conducting leading-edge research. And while it may be true that most university researchers gain their expertise conducting basic research, it is certainly not true to say that these individuals do not have an impact on the productivity or commercialization of applied R&D. The great value placed on the generation of new knowledge is demonstrated by the interactive and symbiotic relationship between basic research and applied R&D. This is because knowledge, as embodied in wetware and software, is increasingly an important factor in economic growth.

Economic growth theory and university R&D

While the benefits of university research outlined in the previous section may seem self-evident, the challenge is to provide a framework for quantifying the multidimensional impact of university research on intellectual capital creation and human capital development. This can best be done using the new economic growth theory.

For years, economists attributed long run economic growth to the two primary factors of production, labour and capital. When the stocks of these variables increased, per capita GDP would grow at a rate equal to their rate of growth.[12] The result of this classical growth model was an economy that would eventually reach a point where it could not grow any faster or, in the jargon, had reached a 'steady state'. This classical model was found to be lacking because it could not explain the tremendous rates of economic growth experienced by numerous countries around the world, particularly after the Second World War. It became apparent that a crucial element of economic growth was missing from the model – technological change.

Technological change allows per capita GDP to increase without increasing the stock of capital or the amount of labour because it makes existing labour and capital more productive. Productivity increases were incorporated into the classical growth model as 'technological change', resulting in the neoclassical growth model. Technological change was considered to be an 'exogenous' factor affecting per capita GDP, where exogenous refers to the fact that the rate of technological change is determined outside the model using econometric techniques. Thus, technological change was a predetermined value that was not influenced by the decisions of firms or individuals. However, this was found to be unsatisfactory because it assumed that individuals and firms have no impact on the rate of technological change, nor on the growth rate of the economy.

In the mid-1980s, growth theorists, led by Paul Romer, hypothesized that knowledge accumulation (particularly through human capital development) was just as important to economic growth as the traditional factors of production. Rather than being some predetermined value, the accumulation of knowledge was influenced by government policy and the decisions of individuals and firms. Hence, models were developed that had four factors of production: labour and capital plus firm-level knowledge and aggregate technological knowledge.[13] These models, known as endogenous growth models, were revolutionary in two ways. First, each extra unit of aggregate knowledge was more and more productive (known as increasing returns),[14] contrary to labour and capital where each extra unit was less and less productive. Second, knowledge was put inside the models – endogenized – recognizing that individuals and firms (economic agents) can affect the rate at which technical knowledge accumulates. Each agent makes a decision as to how much wetware and software it will accumulate from R&D, education and learning by doing. This knowledge decision determines the future productivity of each firm or person, and has a small effect on the productivity of the entire economy since overall GDP growth depends on economy-wide knowledge (which is the sum of all agents' knowledge).

Unfortunately, these models have been difficult to test empirically because much intellectual capital creation is informal, the result of training, learning by doing and learning by using. To complicate matters further, there are no reliable and generally accepted ways to measure wetware and software, let alone concepts such as the stock of technological knowledge, human capital, the cost of knowledge acquisition, the rate of innovation, the rate of obsolescence of old knowledge, etc.[15] Since activities such as R&D have significant impacts on economic growth, these models have important implications for government policy. Current government policies that affect individuals' and firms' decisions to accumulate knowledge have very large consequences on future long run growth rates.

While the empirical limitations of endogenous growth theory have been well chronicled, there is little doubt that the theoretical concepts behind the model are fundamentally sound. In the age of information, development and dissemination of knowledge has been a factor of paramount importance in explaining economic growth. The theoretical underpinnings of the endogenous growth model take into account the profound influence that technological change and innovation have on economic growth. Given its focus on knowledge, the endogenous growth model provides the tools required to measure the benefits to economic growth of an investment in university research activities.

Measuring the dynamic impact of university R&D activities

The dynamic impact is the effect university research has on the productivity and economic growth of the Canadian economy, with wetware and software being the primary propagation mechanisms by which universities affect the economy. Four steps are required to measure the dynamic impact of university research on the Canadian economy. The first is to confirm that there is a strong relation between R&D and productivity, and this is done using regression analysis. Because the results of a regression point only to correlation and not causation, our second step is to use the previously mentioned endogenous growth models to establish a strong theoretical link between R&D and productivity, and then between productivity and GDP growth. The third and fourth steps involve using a model to determine the contribution of knowledge to a change in GDP and then to allocate a portion of this contribution solely to university R&D.

Correlation between R&D, productivity and GDP

Regression analysis is a statistical technique that allows one to determine whether certain variables correlate with each other. For example, a regression of R&D on GDP might reveal that a permanent increase in R&D spending of 1 per cent of GDP today would increase Canadian GDP by 18 per cent in the future.[16] However, simply saying that two variables are correlated does not imply that one necessarily causes the other to change. Unless independent causation is established, it would be wrong in this example to say that a change in R&D causes an increase in GDP. In fact, the new growth models suggest that R&D does not have a direct effect on economic growth, but that R&D – more specifically, the 'wetware' and 'software' that comes from R&D expenditures – increases the productivity of human and physical capital which in turn increases GDP.

To determine whether R&D and productivity vary together, a regression analysis involving 22 OECD countries, using output per employee (GDP/E) as the measure of productivity is conducted.[17] The results, provided in detail in Appendix A, suggest that increases in R&D explain 56 per cent of the increase in productivity, which in turn leads to higher GDP. This value shows that there is a significant correlation between R&D and productivity and eventually GDP, but we are now left to establish causation.

Establishing causation and quantifying the contribution of domestic R&D expenditure

In order to infer causation, we need to establish, using intuition and formal models, that university R&D causes an increase in Canadian GDP. Graphically, we wish to show that:

R&D → knowledge and technology → productivity increases → higher GDP[18]

We can begin this exercise by determining which factors influence GDP. From the section on growth theory it has been established that labour, capital and intermediate inputs (such as natural resources) are the prime determinants of the level of GDP. However, the stocks of wetware and software (knowledge) have an indirect effect on GDP because they create economic growth by making other inputs more productive.

To finish the chain of causation, it is left to define the sources of the knowledge and technology that lead to increased productivity and higher GDP. Knowledge and technology has three sources: it is accumulated from foreign imports of intellectual capital and technology, from imports of goods and services, or it originates from domestic R&D conducted by firms, governments and universities. Thus, we have established that R&D results in knowledge and technology which increases productivity which in turn results in GDP growth. This completes a very informal 'proof' of the causal link between R&D and GDP growth.[19]

Determining the actual effect of R&D on GDP growth involves breaking down the chain of causation into an analytical format that is both quantifiable and amenable to measurement with available data. The model developed in Appendix B, in combination with analytical work and data from the OECD, provides an effective solution. This process involves allocating a portion of the average rate of GDP growth between 1971 and 1993 to total factor productivity (TFP). Much work has been done in this area, providing some reasonably accurate estimates. Given that the average annual real growth rate for Canada has been put at 3.25 per cent by the OECD, and TFP is estimated to contribute 20 per cent of GDP growth (growth in the stocks of labour and capital account for the rest), then the contribution of knowledge (indirectly through TFP) to the Canadian GDP is $73.085304 billion.[20]

The next step involves allocating TFP to its principal components: domestic R&D, foreign R&D and foreign trade. In order to determine the allocation of each of these sources of knowledge and technology, we employ a conservative estimate derived from three independent studies. First, the OECD publishes reliable estimates of the contribution of domestic R&D expenditures to Canadian GDP growth in *Technology, Productivity and Job Creation* (OECD 1996a) in which they estimate that 42 per cent of Canadian TFP originates outside Canada (presumed to include R&D spillovers and trade). Bayoumi et al., in their 1996 study entitled *R&D Spillovers and Global Growth* estimate that 21 per cent of TFP originates in foreign countries, with a small contribution arising from foreign trade. Mohnen (1992) provides a much broader range, suggesting that, depending on the country, between 25 and 65 per cent of TFP can be allocated to foreign sources. Using these three studies, we estimate that only 31 per cent of Canadian total factor productivity can be attributed to foreign R&D.[21] Consequently, Canadian R&D is responsible for 69 per cent of the increases in GDP between 1971 and 1993, or $50.429 billion of Canada's 1993 GDP.

Quantifying the contribution of university R&D

While its exact role in knowledge production and dissemination is difficult to measure precisely, it is apparent that university research has an important influence on knowledge and technology use in the private sector. Anecdotal evidence of this impact comes from studies such as the one conducted on behalf of the National Science Foundation in the United States.[22] This study found that 52 per cent of scientific papers cited on industrial patents have a university source and that 73 per cent of cited papers have various sources of public funds as their source. Given that the private sector conducts less R&D in Canada and is far more dependent on university researchers (see Note 10), it is safe to conclude that university research is just as, if not more, important to the innovative capacity of the Canadian private and public sectors.

A more rigorous method to determine the actual impact of university R&D activities on Canadian productivity involves isolating the effects of two interrelated impacts: the differential productivity of university graduates and the effect on the productivity of other economic agents. Universities' share in the additional productivity of university graduates is measured by calculating graduates' current productivity less their productivity had they not gone to university. This value is put at $2.746 billion per year.[23]

In order to calculate the contribution of university R&D to the higher productivity of other economic agents, we begin with the increase in GDP attributed to knowledge, i.e. $50.4288 billion.[24] From this we must deduct the differential salaries and wages paid to university graduates, as mentioned in the previous paragraph, leaving a total contribution of knowledge to GDP of $42.581 billion. Given that university research directly accounts for approximately 30 per cent of R&D in Canada, this amount can also be used to calculate the relative impact of university research on GDP. Therefore, university research accounts for 30 per cent of the $42.581 billion increase in GDP attributable to knowledge, equal to $12.774 billion.

Add the increases in GDP imputable to universities arising from graduates with higher productivity and the total impact of university R&D on the Canadian economy is $15.521 billion. This represents a $7.5 addition to GDP for every $1 invested in university research by the federal government.

Conclusion

It is somewhat paradoxical that activities like university research and training, which have arguably the most significant impact on the knowledge-based economies, have until recently been virtually unquantifiable. Most economists and analysts will agree that measuring the economic impact of a particular industry or project is difficult. This analysis builds on the fact that as Canada's major source of new knowledge, university research has a fundamental, long-term impact on the overall productivity of the economy. In an age where economic growth is increasingly driven by knowledge generation, these results underline the fact that university research activities must be seen as indispensable in a knowledge intensive, globally competitive marketplace. Consequently, university research has a significant and crucial role to play in Canada's economic prosperity, as predicted by the new growth theory on which this work is founded.

Appendix A

The regression takes the form:

$$\log Y_{it} = \log \alpha + \log X_{it-1} + \log e_t^{25}$$

where:
- i = country
- t = year (1993 for R&D and 1994 for productivity)
- Y_{it} = productivity measured by GDP (at purchasing power parity)/population
- α = constant
- β = slope of logarithmic relation
- X_{it-1} = R&D/population
- e_t = error term

The results of the regression are:

$$\log Y_{it} = 9.26 + 0.209816 \log X_{it-1} \quad R^2 = 0.563409$$
$$\text{Std error of coefficient} = 0.0413$$

Appendix B

As established in the section on endogenous growth theory, GDP is determined by not only the neoclassical factors of production, labour (L) and capital (K), but also by total factor productivity (TFP), which in turn is determined by the stock of technology and scientific knowledge. A standard national production function relating GDP to these factors of production would take the form:[26]

Equation 1

$$Y = FK^{\alpha}L^{1-\alpha} \quad 0 < \alpha > 1$$

where:
- Y = GDP
- F = total factor productivity (TFP)
- L = labour
- K = physical capital.

Since we are actually trying to relate knowledge to GDP through the intermediate variable of productivity growth, Equation 1 is augmented so that TFP is now a product of knowledge and other intermediate variables. Furthermore, the production function is transformed into a growth equation so that all variables are expressed as rates of growth:[27]

Equation 2

$$\Delta TFP = \frac{(\rho-1)}{\beta\rho}(\alpha l + \$m + .k) + \phi_t + \mu r + \psi s$$

where ΔTFP = change in total factor productivity
ρ = an index of returns to scale (ρ = 1 means constant returns to scale)
",$,. = production elasticities of rates of growth of production factors
l,m,k = production factors
φ = rate of technological change
r,s = rates of growth of scientific capital and of its spillovers
μ,ψ = elasticities of production of scientific capital and spillovers.

Assuming constant returns to scale, it can be shown that:

Equation 3

$$TFP = \phi_t + \mu r + \psi s$$

Equation 3 establishes a clear causal relationship between productivity and knowledge since productivity is written as a function of knowledge – that is, TFP depends on φ. Given that it has also been shown that GDP growth is a function of TFP (see Equation 1), it has been proven that GDP growth is also dependent on research and development.

Appendix C: calculation of the portion of 1993 Canadian GDP allocated to growth in TFP

The calculations are based on the average rate of growth of Canadian GDP between the years 1971 and 1990, as compiled by the OECD. It is assumed that this average real rate of growth also holds for the years up to 1993 so that the total number of years is 22.

Average real rate of growth 1971–90 = 3.25%
Canadian GDP in 1971 (in 1986 $) = $286.998 billion
Canadian GDP in 1993 (in 1986 constant dollars) is $580.042 billion, that is:
1.0325 × $286.998 billion = $580.042 billion
Therefore, the increase in GDP from 1971 to 1993 in constant 1986 dollars is:
$580.042 billion – $286.998 billion = $293.044 billion
In 1993 dollars, we use the GDP price index:
$293.044 × 1.247 = $365.42652 billion
Of which, 20 per cent of the growth is attributable to growth in TFP:
20% × $365.42652 = $73.085304 billion

Thus, the portion of Canadian GDP in 1993 attributable to growth in TFP, which is derived from knowledge and technological progress, is $73.085 billion. Note that this somewhat underestimates the effect of TFP on GDP growth because we do not credit any increases in GDP before 1971 to TFP. Furthermore, using OECD or other estimates would ascribe a higher percentage of GDP growth to technological progress. For example, using the OECD Divisia method would allocate 25 per cent to TFP, which would yield a result of $91.36 billion. These estimates are therefore quite conservative.

Appendix D

The additional productivity of higher degree graduates is measured by their differential income. Statistics Canada (1994: 13–217) calculates that the average income of a person with a university degree is $58,787 per year for men and $41,730 per year for women; with a resulting overall average of $51,787 per year. This compares to those in the category below university graduate, who have an average annual income of $36,711 per year. Therefore, the differential income from obtaining a university degree is $15,076 per year.

Increases in average incomes, taking into consideration the working life of individuals, are greater for graduate, postgraduate and professions degree holders, as well as generally higher for men compared to women. For men, Hecker (1995) puts the increase in income of a BA graduate at $4000 less than the average increase in income of all degrees. For MA degrees, the increase in income is $3000 more than the average. Results are significantly greater for professional degrees, but their small numbers minimizes their relative importance.

We therefore put the differential income of MAs and professional degrees at $4924 over the differential in income due to an undergraduate university degree. Thus, the average income of MA and professional degree holders is $36,771 + ($15,076 + $4924) = $56,711.

The average income of BA degree holders is calculated as follows:

The average of *all* university graduates (i.e. BA + MA + Ph.D. + professional degree holders) is $15,076 × $2,419,750[28] = $36,479,751,000

Given that MA and professional degree holders account for $16,679,500,000, the remainder belongs to BA degree holders, equal to approximately $12,500 per BA graduate, or equivalent to an income of $36,711 + $12,500 = $49,211.

A higher degree therefore provides a differential of income over a BA degree of $7500. This represents the net contribution of graduate studies and, by our assumption, the R&D knowledge transmitted to these degree holders. While R&D is not necessary to teach BA students, we assume that professors conducting R&D augment the quality of the teaching and that undergraduate students will benefit, again through a higher quality degree, from the better facilities and equipment provided for research (such as libraries, laboratories and leading-edge equipment).

Consequently, accounting for the contribution of R&D activities to BA degrees involves crediting one-quarter of the increase in income (productivity) to R&D, i.e. 25 per cent of $12,500, or $3125. For Canada as a whole, the increase in productivity of university graduates is therefore:

833,975 (graduates with higher degrees) × $7500 = $6,254,812,500
1,585,775 (BA degree holders only)   × $3125 = $4,955,546,875
                                               $11,210,359,375

But, as shown previously, only 70 per cent of this amount can be imputed directly to domestic R&D since 30 per cent of knowledge is from foreign sources. Consequently, the addition to GDP resulting from a change in knowledge originating in universities is:

$11,210,359,375 × 0.7 = $7.84725 billion

Measuring the Economic Impact 61

However, this amount cannot be entirely credited to the universities since this increase in productivity (due to the generation and transfer of knowledge) is the result of two contributing factors:

1. students who contribute tuition fees, subsistence expenditures and foregone income (for those that study full time); and
2. university expenditures.

The expenditures of each contributing factor to the share of universities is 35 per cent. The total contribution of university R&D to the change in GDP is then:

$7.84725 × 0.35 = $2.74654 billion

Appendix E

In the section on establishing causation and quantifying the contribution of domestic R&D (see page 55), the contribution of knowledge in general was established to be $73.1 billion (corresponding to the value of the effect of TFP). Part of this amount is allocated to foreign sources such that the remaining increase in GDP from access to domestic Canadian knowledge is $50.428859 billion. This amount is redistributed according to the Canadian economic structure, which translates into:

Salaries and wages in the portion of GDP attributable to knowledge (billion Cdn $):		
50.428859 × 0.5675		28.618377
minus already allocated university graduates salaries and wages (Cdn $)		−7.847252
sub-total		20.771125
plus other revenues	50.428859 × 0.1839	+21.810481
total unallocated		**$42.581606**

As previously mentioned, a reasonable but imperfect basis to allocate this amount to university research is to use its relative importance with respect to all R&D in Canada, i.e. 30 per cent. The share of universities' R&D is then:

$42.851606 × $0.30 = $12.74481 billion

The total contribution of university R&D to the change in GDP is then:

its contribution to the human capital (billion Cdn $)	2.746538
its contribution to other economic agents (billion Cdn $) total	12.774481
total	**15.521019**

This represents a return of roughly $7.5 for each dollar invested by government in university research.

Notes

1. The Statistics Canada Canadian Interprovincial Open I-O Model is a detailed accounting framework representing the whole of the Canadian economy. The model is 'static' in that the productivity of the factors of production, and the structure of the economy in general, is not changed by the characteristics of

the simulation project being run through the Statistics Canada model. It is 'gross' in the sense that all expenditures are considered new; that is, they would not have been made had the project in question not taken place. 'Open' refers to the fact that the Statistics Canada simulation only measures the first and second round spending impacts, as opposed to a closed model which would calculate the full impact of the Keynesian multiplier. Data is taken from Statistics Canada and Canadian Association of University Business Officers (CAUBO) sources.

2. The numbers in Table 4.1 are net of the indirect taxes taken in by government because these taxes would be taken in no matter which sector had spent the money. That is to say, the funds cannot be attributed solely to university research. However, many economic impact studies would include this amount as part of their economic impact of a particular project. The amount of indirect taxes is:

From university R&D	0.503
From students' expenditures	0.061
Total	$0.564 billion

3. In Canada, research expenditures represent about one-fifth of total university spending.
4. The government investment in university research must be financed by raising taxes, borrowing (which increases interest rates) or by cutting government spending elsewhere. Given that the Statistics Canada Model cannot account for these, we must adjust the results of the I-O estimation to provide realistic results. This step is very frequently omitted in other economic impact studies because it often takes away much of the benefit of a project or activity.
5. Since the results appear modest, the reader may ask why present the gross economic impact. The reason is to enable a preliminary comparison of the impact of R&D university expenditures with the gross impact of rival commercial projects which usually do not pursue the analysis up to the static net impact. Note that still being positive at the level of the static net impact is a very good point in favour of university research. It removes the implications arising from being subsidized.
6. These terms and the definitions that follow are taken from Nelson and Romer (1996).
7. Nelson and Romer (1996: 15).
8. The increase in the productivity of the factors of production (the intermediate inputs used to create the final goods and services that make up GDP) is measured in terms of total factor productivity (TFP). TFP is measured using analytical methods that determine the causes of GDP growth not imputable to simple increases in the labour force, the amount of capital, more natural resources, etc. TFP measures increases in the efficiency of these inputs.
9. OECD (1996b: 23).
10. It is important here to address the myth that university researchers work in an ivory tower completely divorced from the needs of the private sector. By any measure, Canadian industry is more dependent on university labs than industry in almost any other OECD country. The fact is that universities in Canada conduct more industry-sponsored research, as a percentage of total R&D, than universities in most OECD nations. In recent years, the percentage of industry-sponsored research has varied between 18 and 20 per cent. A possible reason is that very few private sector firms in Canada have large-scale research facilities,

such that many firms use the leading-edge equipment and facilities on Canadian university campuses.
11. A 1998 study by the Natural Sciences and Engineering Research Council of Canada (NSERC 1998) suggests that 106 companies, with over $1.1 billion in annual sales and employing almost 6000 people, were created from NSERC-funded research and researchers.
12. However, extra amounts of capital and labour were seen to be less and less productive – known as decreasing marginal returns. This implies that an economy cannot grow without bound by increasing only one of these inputs. Eventually, since each extra unit produces less and less, additional inputs will have a zero marginal contribution to output, resulting in no growth.
13. Aggregate knowledge is considered to be an externality – that is, when a firm produces knowledge, that knowledge becomes publicly available and so increases the knowledge available to other firms as well. One can therefore see how a firm's productivity would depend not only on its stock of knowledge but on the economy-wide stock of knowledge (as well as labour and capital).
14. This assumption means that an economy could theoretically grow without bound, since each extra unit of intellectual capital will add a larger amount to GDP.
15. Howitt (1996: 4).
16. These numbers are not accidental, they are the results of a study conducted by Bayoumi *et al.* (1996). In their study, Canada was the country for which the greatest increase in GDP would result from an increase in R&D expenditures, providing more evidence of the critical role knowledge plays in the Canadian economy.
17. The purpose of this regression is only to show that there is a relationship between R&D and productivity. While many other factors also affect GDP growth, such as the state of the physical infrastructure (airports, roads, etc.), labour force participation, natural resource endowments and the relatively high R-squared of the regression results suggest that this relationship does in fact exist.
18. This approach appears to correspond to the linear research model. New models of research suggest that research represents a continuum with many feedback loops, blurring the distinction between basic and applied research. Since we do not need to distinguish between basic and applied research, our calculations are compatible with all types of research model.
19. A proper proof would require this to be done algebraically. This is supplied in Appendix B.
20. See Appendix C for detailed calculations.
21. The rationale for using 31 per cent is that we use the average of the OECD and Bayoumi *et al.* (1996) estimates (including 2 per cent for foreign trade and spillovers), while ensuring that it meets the minimum of the Mohnen (1992) estimates.
22. Narin *et al.* (1997).
23. See Appendix D for detailed calculations.
24. As previously discussed, knowledge is embodied in other economic agents, making them more productive and thereby increasing GDP. Consequently, to determine the differential impact on these other variables, we use their relative importance in Canadian GDP. Thus, salaries and wages make up 56.75 per cent of GDP, other income (business profits, interest, etc.) accounts for 18.39 per cent while taxes, subsidies and depreciation account for the remaining 24.86 per cent. Salaries therefore account for 56.75 per cent of the $50 billion, equal to $28.618 billion.

From this must be deducted the already accounted for increase in salary attributed to university graduates (see Appendix D), leaving $20.71 billion. Added to the salary total is the share of increased productivity attributed to the other determinants of GDP, giving a total of $42.581 billion.
25. The logarithmic form is used to reduce statistical problems that arise with cross-sectional and time series data, particularly simultaneity and multicollinearity.
26. A model representing the endogenous growth theory might incorporate another variable, Z, which would represent higher productivity of intermediate inputs caused by lower costs or higher quality of these goods from previous improvements in productivity.
27. This model is taken from Bernstein (1996: 395).
28. According to Statistics Canada, in Canada there are currently 883,975 higher degrees and 1,585,775 BA degree holders.

References

Bayoumi, T., Coe, D.T. and Helpman, E. (1996) *R&D Spillovers and Global Growth*, Working Paper no. 79. Toronto, The Canadian Institute for Advanced Research.

Bernstein, J.I. (1996) The Canadian communication equipment industry as a source of R&D spillovers and productivity growth, in P. Howitt *The Implications of Knowledge-Based Growth for Micro-Economic Policies*. Calgary, Alberta, University of Calgary Press, 391–411.

Grady, P. and Muller, R.A. (1986) *On the Use and Misuse of Input-Output Based Impact Analysis in Evaluation*, Research Report no. 185. Hamilton, Ontario, McMaster University.

Hecker, D.E. (1995) The earnings of college graduates, 1993. *Monthly Labor Review*, 188(12): 3–17.

Howitt, P. (1996) *The Implications of Knowledge-Based Growth for Micro-Economic Policies*. Calgary, Alberta, University of Calgary Press.

Mohnen, P. (1992) *The Relationship Between R&D and Productivity Growth in Canada and Other Major Industrialized Countries*. Ottawa, Ontario, Minister of Supply and Services Canada.

Murphy, R.A. (1996) Government policy and university science: starving the golden goose. Killam Address, Canadian Association of Graduate Studies, University of Calgary, 1 November.

Narin, F., Hamilton, K. and Olivastro, D. (1997) The increasing linkage between US technology and public science. *Research Policy*, 26(3), 317.

Nelson, R. and Romer, P. (1996) Science economic growth and public policy. *Challenge*, March–April, 9–21.

NSERC (1998) *Data Brief: Spin-off Companies*. Ottawa, Ontario, NSERC.

OECD (Organization for Economic Cooperation and Development) (1994) *Statistics on the Member Countries*. Supplement to the OECD *Observer* no. 188, June/July. Paris, OECD.

OECD (Organization for Economic Cooperation and Development) (1996a) *Technology, Productivity and Job Creation*, vol. 2, Analytical Report. Paris, OECD.

OECD (Organization for Economic Cooperation and Development) (1996b) *Oslo Manual*, 2nd edition (October). Paris, OECD.

Poole, E. (1993) *A Guide to Using the Input-Output Model of Statistics Canada*. 58E, Technical Series. Ottawa, Statistics Canada.

Poole, E., Rioux, R. and Simard, C. (1994) 'The input-output model, employment and impact on economic policy decision making', Manuscript. Ottawa, Ontario, 11 April.

Statistics Canada (1994) Earnings of Men and Women. Ottawa, Ontario, Statistics Canada.

Statistics Canada (1997) *Canada Year Book*. Ottawa, Ontario, Statistics Canada.

5

The Changing Relationship Between Higher Education and Small and Medium Sized Enterprises

Martin Binks

Introduction

Recent trends have conspired to bring together what at first appear rather uncomfortable partners, universities and small and medium sized enterprises (SMEs). Quite independently of each other, the trends have been highly significant in their strength and have profound implications each for the other if UK competitiveness is to be sustained.

The 'massification' of higher education (HE) has been accompanied by a growing emphasis upon its economic contribution. The threefold increase in the number of graduates between 1977 and 1995 has coincided with fundamental and irreversible changes in the labour market. The development of new funding arrangements has reorientated or 'disorientated' the strategies of individual universities and altered their approach to teaching and learning and also to research. There is also evidence of a changing relationship between HE and industry. Although ultimately driven by financial factors, this reflects the increased emphasis upon relevance and economic contribution which has developed in recognition of the crucial role which high level skills will play in retaining comparative advantage over growing international competition.

The increasing focus upon the economic contribution of SMEs in the UK can be traced back to the report of the Committee of Enquiry on Small Firms chaired by John Bolton which reported in November 1971 (Bolton 1971). A prodigious amount of research was required before the Bolton Committee could make confident judgements about the SME sector because of its almost complete neglect by previous generations of economists, sociologists, geographers and politicians. The focus upon SMEs increased gradually during the 1970s. Having started at such a low level of interest, it was not until the late 1970s that 'critical mass' in terms of public and political awareness was achieved, and this accelerated the SME issue up the political agenda. Cynics would argue, largely correctly, that at first the attention lavished on SMEs owed more to the inability of large firms to absorb rapidly rising levels of unemployment than to an explicit belief in their particular and economically valuable characteristics. If the emphasis upon SMEs had been driven entirely by negative forces, then it would eventually have dissipated as their actual capacity for employment creation became clearer. This did not occur, however, because more positive aspects of 'entrepreneurship' and SME characteristics attracted attention during the 1980s and 1990s (Stanworth and Grey 1991). The significant growth in the number of SMEs was caused primarily by a large increase in micro-businesses. Entrepreneurship and SMEs are now permanent and established features of the political and economic agenda and like the massification of HE, are regarded as a crucial element in the pursuit of international competitiveness (e.g. HMSO 1994).

The coincidence of these trends in HE and the SME sector has produced a simple rationale for encouraging links between the two. The increase in the number of graduates has not been accompanied by a corresponding rise in graduate recruitment by large businesses. Recruitment problems in large firms are caused largely by shortages of graduates with the appropriate skills and competencies rather than an absolute shortage *per se* (Barclays Commercial Services 1997; DfEE 1997). To gain employment many graduates will find jobs with SMEs. The rapid pace of technological change means that many SMEs require graduate-level skills merely to keep up with the competition. Rapidly changing international competitiveness as a result of the industrialization process in China, India and other areas of the Far East is based upon low wage, competitive advantage. High technology SMEs with highly skilled workforces are seen as a vital component in the UK's strategy towards sustained competitiveness under these changing conditions. The rationale for encouraging partnerships between HE and SMEs would appear to be indisputable. Graduates need SMEs for employment; their high level skills and competencies are needed by those firms in order to remain competitive, and the UK needs those firms to remain competitive as part of its overall competitiveness agenda.

This simple rationale is attractive because it is convincing as long as the debate is restricted to discussions around aggregates such as 'HE' and 'SMEs'. The problems of realizing this vision in practice and designing strategies and policies to achieve it can only be appreciated from a more disaggregated perspective. The aim of this chapter is to consider the SME and HE sectors to ascertain the potential for effective partnerships in practice. Having considered each sector in terms of its evolution, present agendas and drivers and the scope, extent and nature of such partnerships in the future can be more clearly identified.

The SME sector

Virtually all firms in the UK are small: 97.6 per cent of firms employ less than 20 people. The terms small, medium and large have been variously

68 *Martin Binks*

Table 5.1 Composition of the small firm sector

	Micro (0–9)	Small (10–99)	**Total (<100)**	Size (number of employees) Medium (100–499)	Large (500+)	**All Firms**
Total	3,502,304	188,267	**3,690,571**	12,416	3091	**3,706,078**

Source: DTI Statistics Bulletin, June 1995a.

Figure 5.1 UAT registration and deregistration series

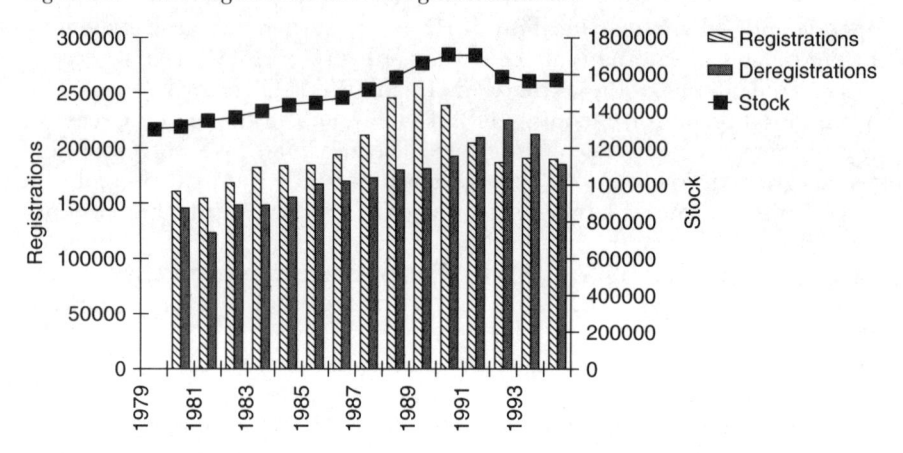

Source: National Westminster Bank 1996.

defined in terms of employment, turnover and asset values. It is unnecessary here to adopt a rigid definition and some of the data which follow are categorized according to different measures. As a general rule of thumb, it might be sensible to assume that small firms have a turnover of less than £1 million and medium sized businesses less than £10 million. In terms of employment, a small firm might employ less than 100 people and a medium sized firm less than 500. The distribution of SMEs by size is shown in Table 5.1.

The distribution of business between sectors varies through time and the particular skills and competencies required of the workforce vary significantly between sectors and also over time. In order to predict future skill requirements it is necessary to forecast accurately the changing levels of economic activity by sector and changing needs within the sectors. Throughout the 1980s there was a steady increase in the stock of businesses as indicated by the VAT registration and deregistration series (see Figure 5.1). There was also a significant rise in self-employment (see Figure 5.2).

Aside from variations by size and sector there are also large differences between businesses in terms of their age, growth potential, management

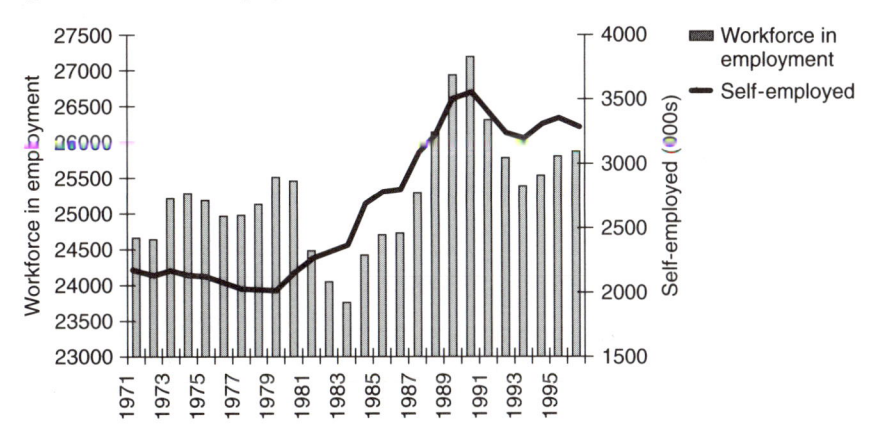

Figure 5.2 UK self-employment

Source: National Westminster Bank 1996.

style, profitability, expectations, technological awareness, technological sophistication and many other business characteristics. In short, in many contexts it is misleading and counter-intuitive to refer to 'the SME sector'. The vast majority of small firms do not involve high technology; most deal with local markets and have little in the way of significant growth potential. It is important to recognize this huge diversity of characteristics and needs when considering the relationship between SMEs and HE in aggregate.

Policy and SMEs

Prior to the Bolton Report (Bolton 1971) it was largely the case that small firms in the UK were regarded as undesirable. The conventional wisdom had it that without economies of scale or size they must be less efficient than large firms. As other sources of efficiency were identified in the 1970s and after, the picture appeared less clear. For example, in terms of organizational efficiency, flexibility and responsiveness, it appeared that small size could be an advantage. Focus was then directed at the design of policies to overcome certain natural but undesirable disadvantages also associated with smaller firms.

A plethora of policy measures has been introduced since the Bolton Report in 1971. These have referred to the provision of information to SMEs, the delivery of appropriate skills and training, and a wide variety of financial and related initiatives.

The concerns and skills needs of SMEs

In terms of their own perceptions of constraints upon their activities, SMEs are relatively consistent in their views as demonstrated by Figure 5.3 which shows the predominant concern with levels of market demand but also a

Figure 5.3 Selected most important problems

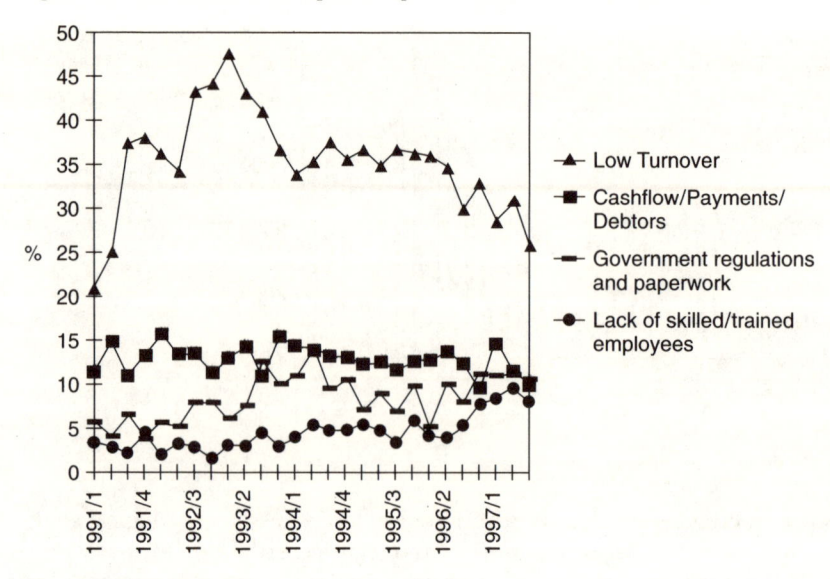

[Chart showing percentages from 1991/1 to 1997/1 for: Low Turnover, Cashflow/Payments/Debtors, Government regulations and paperwork, Lack of skilled/trained employees]

Source: Small Business Research Trust 1997.

consistent recognition of skills shortages. This perception is supported by evidence from other sources such as the Skills and Enterprise Network which reported on skills needs in Britain in 1996 (DfEE 1997) and found significant shortfalls in information technology (IT) skills and a growing recognition by firms of the need for employee training.

There is a shortage of accurate, up-to-date information on skills needs, however, making the task of those responsible for their delivery, such as the Training and Enterprise Councils (TECs), problematic. Aside from previous experience the main sources of information upon which training providers can rely refer usually to their own labour market intelligence surveys and predictions of groups such as Cambridge Econometrics in their 'Regional Economic Projects'.

The shortage of reliable, accurate and up-to-date information and training is seen to cause severe market failure. PA Cambridge Economic Consultants, in their evaluation of Department of Trade and Industry (DTI) funded TEC services in 1995 (DTI 1995b: 3) concluded that:

- market failure continues to be widespread in the small firm sector
- the free market, in the form of the private sector suppliers of services, has not provided a range of customised services to address that market failure
- DTI funded, TEC delivered services, locally designed and delivered and increasingly customised to small firms' needs, do address important aspects of market failure and in doing so generate significant benefits to small firms and to the wider economy.

The development of sophisticated skills-needs monitoring systems will be a low key element in the transformation of the relationship between HE and SMEs. The transformation itself will be driven by the need for 'lifelong learning' to move from rhetoric to reality.

The SME agenda

The vast majority of SMEs at present are probably preoccupied most by short-term issues and, for many, deciding the most appropriate strategy to survive into the medium term. Most owner-managers have never been to university or had any contact with HE. The key drivers and concerns are short-term economic prospects and conditions. For an important minority, however, evidence from programmes such as the STEP (Shell Technology and Enterprise Programme) initiative and many others suggest that significant potential benefits can accrue to both firms and graduates by bringing the two together. The most appropriate strategies for encouraging this process will be considered after the next section, which provides pertinent observations on the previous and present state of HE in the UK.

The HE sector

The changing conditions in HE in the UK in terms of research output, numbers of students, skills provision, access, accreditation, finance and a wide variety of other characteristics are well rehearsed and have been well documented not least in the 1997 National Committee of Enquiry into Higher Education Report (The Dearing Report) (NCIHE 1997). For the purposes of this chapter it is sufficient to restrict coverage and focus to a few of the most relevant points. These refer to the variety of conditions within HE, the shift in policy towards the sector and the present emphasis in teaching and learning developments and research.

Variety within HE: the example of the East Midlands

A good illustration of the wide differences between institutions in HE can be gained by considering conditions in a single region. There are 11 HE institutions in the East Midlands region (including the Open University). In 1996/7 they attracted 124,467 students, 92,913 full-time and 31,554 part-time. HE in the region is an 'attractive' force and well-qualified young people move into the region to study in large numbers. Table 5.2 illustrates the range of HE institutions in the East Midlands by numbers of students and shows that HE providers in the region vary between small specialist colleges, median range research universities and large, predominantly teaching universities (see Table 5.3).

Table 5.2 HE student numbers in the East Midlands region (1996/7)

Universities and Colleges	Full-time undergraduate students	Part-time undergraduate students	Full-time postgraduate students	Part-time postgraduate students	Other undergraduates	Total students
Bishop Gs College	795	0	20	24	9	730
Derby University**	7426	772	253	937	2174	11568
De Montfort University**	13128	1697	1123	1685	3023	20656
Leicester University	6729	75	1604	3464	2319	14432
Lincoln and Humberside University*,**	7254	1139	413	687	2171	11664
Loughborough University	7790	82	1140	1509	31	10677
Loughborough College of Art & Design	624	18	0	0	88	730
Nene College	5864	457	218	713	2714	9981
University of Nottingham	9810	112	2102	1336	6054	21062
Nottingham Trent University**	14621	1434	705	1793	4268	22822
Open University*	0	87017	422	18717	18946	125102

* These are total numbers for the Open University and for Lincoln and Humberside; they are not disaggregated by region.
** Post 1992 universities.
Source: HESA 1997.

Table 5.3 Some features of the student population in the East Midlands region (1996)

College/university	Sandwich students	Arts/science ratio	Male/female ratio	% Mature students*
Bishop Gs College	0	100/0	14/86	27
De Montfort University	2991	53/47	54/46	25
Derby University	0	69/31	45/55	38
Leicester University	135	55/45	50/50	15
Lincoln and Humberside**	2824	70/30	50/50	27
Loughborough University	2245	41/59	64/36	17
Nene College	618	62/38	40/60	31
University of Nottingham	0	38/62	55/45	12
Nottingham Trent University	6533	54/46	57/43	18

* Over 21 on entry.
** This is data for the whole university; it is not disaggregated into students in the regions.
Source: HESA 1997.

A further interesting observation which emerges from Table 5.2 concerns the variation in numbers of part-time undergraduates between institutions, with relatively low figures for pre-1992 universities as compared with the post-1992 institutions.

Aside from variations in the size and patterns of the student body in HE, there is also wide variation in the strategies and 'missions' associated with different institutions as a result of significant disparities in their backgrounds and traditions, structures, finances, strengths and weaknesses (Binks and Otter 1997). In short, as with the SME sector, it is misleading and unhelpful to refer to the HE sector as if it is an homogenous entity.

Policy shifts

While recognizing the enormous implications and repercussions which will stem from the policy of mass HE, lower unit funding and quality assessment for both research, and teaching and learning, a significant policy shift for the purposes of the present arguments refers to the growing emphasis upon generic as well as subject-specific skills and competencies by students in HE. Changing labour market conditions and pressures from industry have highlighted the importance of interpersonal skills and competencies as key skills. The extent to which this has been recognized and accommodated within HE has varied widely between institutions but is nevertheless surprising in terms of the speed with which it has been accepted. In some disciplines the need to refocus the curriculum and the way in which it is delivered has been promoted by the accrediting bodies which oversee the activities of the departments and faculties concerned. Pressure has also been generated by organizations such as the Association of Graduate Recruiters (AGR), the Confederation of British Industry (CBI) and the DTI.

In terms of specific policy initiatives, one of the most successful and still influential refers to the Enterprise in Higher Education programme (EHE) which was introduced in 1988, with the cessation of funding support in 1996. The success of EHE was due in part to its timing since it almost anticipated future trends in the labour market and employer requirements rather than responding *ex post facto*. Its design and in particular the flexibility which allowed each participating institution to accommodate its own structures and conditions was also a strong element in its effectiveness. EHE generated a huge number of individual projects within institutions many of which were concerned with links between HE and industry with specific reference often to SMEs. It is from the experience of these and other projects that future strategists can learn when attempting to encourage HE and SMEs to work more closely with each other.

A good example of policy design which is likely to focus on HE and SMEs in the future is the Higher Education Regional Development Fund (HERDF). Although relatively modest at the time of writing it would seem sensible to assume that funding support of this kind will increase as the regionalization process continues and the Regional Development Agencies (RDAs) begin to plan a coordinating role between their own SME populations and the HE providers in their area.

The trend towards encouraging students to acquire generic as well as subject-specific and vocational skills is particularly relevant to the needs of SMEs. Policy initiatives such as EHE along with more recent Department for Education and Employment (DfEE) programmes which encourage work experience and placement activities provide students with the necessary qualifications to work effectively in an SME. SMEs cannot afford lengthy induction courses to enable graduates to make a useful and valuable contribution towards their activities. For SMEs, graduates are required to 'hit the ground running' and start making a contribution shortly after taking up employment.

Although drawn from the experience of large firms, a useful and clear insight to conditions prevailing post-Dearing is provided by Roly Cockman, chief executive of the Association of Graduate Recruiters, in an article published in the *Guardian* in October 1997. Describing the increase in vacancies in large firms he makes the following observations: '. . . the increase in vacancies is expected to be around 18 per cent and follows a steady increase in vacancies over the last three years . . . The result of all this is that, even with the increase in vacancies, employers will probably get about 100 applications for every position they offer. Employers can still afford to be selective, and they are' (Cockman 1997).

The relevance of this to conditions confronting SMEs is first that excess demand for vacancies in large businesses implies a steady supply of graduates who will consider employment in an SME as an alternative. In many cases, however, it is likely that the most 'able' graduates will still be creamed off by large employers. Cockman's next point demonstrates the existence of skill shortages within the context of, and overall surplus in, the supply of graduates. This point is particularly important when confronting those who argue that investment in higher level skills is excessive by citing evidence of an excess supply of graduates: 'There are some areas where it is more difficult to recruit than others. The more able graduates in IT and computing disciplines and in electrical and electronic engineering are comparatively better placed than those trying to enter sales and general management traineeships' (Cockman 1997).

The emphasis upon generic skills and competencies is evidenced clearly in the next paragraph of Cockman's article:

> About half of the vacancies on offer to graduates this year will not specify any particular degree discipline. Employers offering these positions are looking for a reasonable degree and evidence of some academic rigour. They will then probably base their selection on the competencies required to be successful in the first appointment. Research and AGR [Association of Graduate Recruiters] had identified that those likely to be successful are the self-confident and self-reliant.
>
> (Cockman 1997)

The set of generic attributes which attracted much attention in EHE have, according to Cockman, been considered in a more discerning way by employers:

> Traditionally employers of graduates have looked, among other things, for motivation and enthusiasm, good interpersonal skills, team-working, flexibility and good oral and written communication. Lately they have become more sophisticated in their requirements, as a result mainly of the reduction in the number of long training programmes on offer and the need for graduate employees to manage their own careers.
>
> (Cockman 1997)

Many of the attributes which are pushed forward in the article are equally applicable to SMEs as to large firms. If there were an effective and efficient process for encouraging students to acquire these attributes, then their preparedness for work would also encompass SMEs as well as large firms: 'Nowadays, successful graduates need a range of skills which allow them to adapt to changing market circumstances and organisational needs. They need to be aware of the culture of the organisation they are trying to join, so that they can rapidly fit in' (Cockman 1997).

If the views expressed in the article are typical of employers in general and these are communicated to students, then the emphasis upon standards in terms of generic attributes rather than the subject-specific aspects which are also of concern will encourage the development of a workforce suited both to the conditions in SMEs and large firms:

> Surprisingly, although employers receive a large number of applications for most graduate vacancies, many remain unfilled at the end of the

recruitment period. This year, 45 per cent of employers experienced real difficulties in filling all their vacancies, compared with 39 per cent last year. This should send a clear message to graduate applicants. Even though there are more vacancies, if you aren't up to the standard required, you will not be taken on.

(Cockman 1997)

Teaching and learning developments

While key issues vary significantly between institutions, a prime focus for many will refer to funding and the relative balance between increased student numbers and a greater emphasis upon research. Dramatic improvements in the capability of IT to revolutionize distance learning will also become an increasing focus of attention for many institutions, both as an opportunity and a threat to their future activities. Globalization and the effective shrinking of the planet in terms of distances and communications is also causing many institutions to look nationally and internationally as well as regionally and locally.

For many traditional research-led universities, the needs and requirements of SMEs are relatively low on their agenda. However, for many of the more locally and regionally based post-1992 universities there is a much greater awareness of the trends within the SME sector and their relevance to institutional activities. It is important that this imbalance is to some extent counteracted through policies such as the HERDF in order to ensure that SMEs within regions have full access to the potential benefits which the HE sector in the region can provide.

Synthesis

From the above, it is clear that the key influences and 'drivers' for both HE and most SMEs do not involve their relationship with each other. Existing evidence and anticipated future trends suggest that there is mutual benefit to be gained by discerning, selective and often close cooperation between SMEs and HE institutions. The problem confronting HE, SMEs and those responsible for encouraging closer cooperation refers to identifying effective processes which encourage appropriate partnerships to develop without relying upon an overarching general 'scatter-gun' strategy. The danger of an undiscerning and general policy of pressurizing HE and SMEs into partnership activities is that it will cause resentment and resistance to grow in the institutions and SMEs concerned.

It is clear from the above that SMEs will vary significantly in terms of their skills needs. HE also reflects great variety in the provisions available at any one time and the requirements for access. It would be expected, therefore, that successful partnership activities between HE and SMEs would often be quite idiosyncratic rather than general in their characteristics. If partnerships are contrived which do not reflect mutual needs and benefits then, in failing, as they invariably will, they are more likely to engender negative rather than positive attitudes towards future collaborative opportunities.

Models for successful HE/SME partnerships

Placements and work experience

As indicated earlier the STEP Initiative reveals the potential value of students and graduates to SMEs and vice versa. The model is cited by the Dearing Report (NCIHE 1997), which suggests that it should be increased significantly in its application. In 1997 around 1600 undergraduates were gainfully placed in SMEs. This represents less than 1 per cent of the graduates for that year. This is in no way a criticism of the STEP Initiative but rather an indication of the scale of problems which are likely to be met were an attempt made to expand significantly its impact.

In pursuing an effective model of HE/SME partnership it is necessary to identify clearly and precisely the aims and objectives of the exercise and the extent to which lessons can be drawn from previous experience such as STEP and other placement programmes. The aims of such a policy would appear to be twofold. The first is to enable students to acquire the generic and interpersonal skills which they will need to perform effectively in employment after graduation. The second aim is to enable SMEs to gain access to higher level skills and competencies which they need to remain competitive. The key objective is for students to gain work experience in SMEs. A secondary objective is to equip them in such a way that they can appreciate the work experience benefits which this enables.

Developing proactive relationships

While acknowledging the important role of placements and work experience in the skills-based relationship between HE and SMEs there are a growing number of opportunities for collaboration in many other areas.

Lifelong learning capability requires significant changes in the supply side of HE and further education (FE). Widening access has implications for part-time provision and selective accredited participation in modules. Universities which provide skills and knowledge in formats tailored to accommodate the needs and constraints of potential applicants will benefit from high margins on these services. In the case of SMEs this is potentially a very large market as more firms begin to recognize the need for the regular upgrading of the skills and knowledge of their staff. This process of structured change with higher education institutions (HEIs) to create greater flexibility in provision is already in evidence to varying extents in different institutions. Although conditions in post-1992 universities are more conducive to such changes in the short run, as a result of their traditionally closer engagement with the local economy, the balance is likely to alter in the medium term. The existing and often strong links between research-led universities and industry which focus upon technology transfer would, increasingly, be expected to embody stronger skills provision options. Technology transfer often requires a corresponding investment in human capital in order to be effective. With the continual acceleration of technological change, which itself underpins the need for lifelong learning, the emphasis upon high-level skills provision at the forefront of research developments will grow. Although the conventional wisdom tends to associate these developments with large 'hi-tech' firms, many of the firms involved are actually quite small. Aside from the prevalence of SMEs in the 'sunrise industries' there are many in sectors as diverse as financial services, engineering and textiles which are engaged at the forefront of technological development. It is in this context that significant opportunities exist for highly effective partnerships between research-led universities and SMEs.

Key issues

The ability to be selective and discerning requires information which is wide ranging, up to date and available to SMEs, HE institutions and potential students. These information needs refer to regional supply and demand conditions for labour market skills and the underlying influences which cause changes in each. HE provisions vary widely by institution in terms of higher-level skills and technological and research capabilities. Businesses and individuals require different levels of training in different areas at different times. This has implications for modularization and the ability for individuals to gain accreditation from short courses or small parts of larger courses easily and at a cost which they or their employer can afford.

As there is a movement away from the rhetoric of lifelong learning towards effective actions and initiatives to make it a reality for most people, the transparency of the HE sector for individuals and firms will be of increasing importance.

It is also likely that as more SMEs employ graduates and more graduates set up businesses, the traditional mindset of the SME sector which views HE as being of little relevance to its operations will begin to erode. Similarly as policy and funding emphasize regional economic contributions from HE, so the mindset which regards the SME sector as of little relevance or importance to HE institutions will also adjust.

Conclusions and future prospects

With the erosion of prevailing mindsets, the areas of potential mutual benefit for SMEs and HE will become clearer to both parties. Although much of the present emphasis is upon placement and work experience, with some focus upon technology transfer, it is likely that a much broader range of collaborative relationships will emerge, even though these may only involve a relatively small minority of SMEs, in close and sustained partnerships. Similarly, levels of involvement in HE with close partnerships will vary significantly between institutions.

Given the present relatively low levels of partnership which exist, it is likely that the rate of growth of activities will be quite rapid. As evidence of successful partnership activities becomes more prevalent and more widely disseminated, both in HE and the 'SME community', there will be increasing opportunities for both groups to gain from the benefits which can result.

Although policy initiatives will focus to some extent on proven processes and their dissemination, the potential for funds such as the HERDF to enable HE, SMEs and Business Support Agencies to explore new areas of collaboration should not be underestimated. Perhaps one of the most important lessons to be gained from previous experience is that of process rather than structure. The EHE programme did not prescribe a particular structure or model of operation, but rather it encouraged institutions to develop processes which would be most effective in their particular circumstances. By avoiding unnecessary and almost certainly counter-productive preoccupation with structure, it was possible to maintain a very strong commitment to the ultimate aims of the initiative and confront and assess all activities undertaken within the programme in terms of these ultimate aims.

References

Barclays Commercial Services (1997) *Skills Shortages*. London, Barclays.
Binks, M.R. and Otter, S. (1997) Realising the potential contribution of higher education institutions to their regions and communities. Conference paper presented to the EAIR Conference, Warwick, September.
Bolton, J.E. (1971) *Small Firms: Report of the Committee of Enquiry on Small Firms*, Cmnd. 4811. London, HMSO.
Cockman, R. (1997) Rewards keep rising for the chosen few, the *Guardian*, 4 October.
DfEE (1997) *Skills Needs in Britain*. Skills and Enterprise Network. Sudbury, Suffolk, DfEE Publications.
DTI (Department of Trade and Industry) (1995a) *Small Firms in Britain*. London, HMSO.
DTI (Department of Trade and Industry) (1995b) *Evaluation of DTI funded TEC services*. London, HMSO.
HESA (Higher Education Statistics Agency) (1997) Customised data purchase. Bristol, HESA.
HMSO (1994) *Competitiveness: Helping Businesses to Win*, Cm2563. London, HMSO.
National Westminster Bank (1996) *Nat West Review of Small Businesses*, 6(1), June.
NCIHE (National Committee of Enquiry into Higher Education) (1997) *Report of the Committee of Enquiry into the Funding of Higher Education* (the Dearing Report). London, DfEE.
Small Business Research Trust (1997) *National Westminster Bank Review of Small Business Trends*. London, Small Business Research Trust.
Stanworth, J. and Grey, C. (eds) (1991) *Bolton 20 Years On*. London, PCP.

6

The Role of Universities in Economic Growth: the ASEAN Countries

Paul Milne

Introduction

This chapter focuses on the experience of rapid economic growth in countries within the Association of South East Asian Nations (ASEAN) and in particular that of Malaysia and Singapore. The factors which accounted for their successful development have, somewhat ironically, been identified as the very causes of the recent 'meltdown' in East Asia. As noted below, the role of Asian values – especially those which emphasize consensus and respect for authority – together with the heavy inward-flowing capital, large deficits on the current account of balance of payments and extensive government expenditure, finally resulted in a lack of investor confidence in continued sustainable growth. The common opinion of commentators is that recovery to previous levels of activity is unlikely to occur before the year 2000.

Economic development processes

The literature on economic development has displayed marked shifts in emphasis in the last three decades. The optimism displayed in the 1960s that rapid growth could be achieved by the implementation of substantial capital investment and the introduction of modern technology was not to be fulfilled. The new institutional economics school takes, as a starting point, transaction relationships which are critical for the mobilization and shifting of resources. Private and public sector institutions such as business groups linked by communal ethnic or regional groups, networks, business-interest associations and public-private sector consultation groupings are typical examples. However, as Doner (1991) points out, this approach focuses on the demand for such institutions but not the supply. Some type of normative consensus is a precondition. For long-term relationships, for example in South East Asia, the ties among the Chinese community have been critical in the development of credit and business groupings.

This approach runs contrary to the dependency or the institutionalist approaches. The former examines the product life cycle typified by the 'wild flying geese pattern' of Akamatsu (1960), in which the leader of the formation is periodically replaced. The diffusion and spreading of technology occurs as the manufacture of products moves from the initial innovator to countries with less developed technology. Thus Malaysia currently is dominant in electronics with 30 per cent of its exports and 18 per cent of its manufacturing dependent on that sector (Asian Development Bank 1996). The institutionalist approach requires structures which permit effective mobilization and shifting of resources. Protection to encourage import substitution, ineffective market mechanisms and a lack of openness restricts the process in less developed countries.

Economic infrastructure of the region

In 1993 the World Bank policy research report, *The East Asian Miracle* (World Bank 1993) focused on the eight High Performing Asian Economies (HPAEs), namely Japan, the 'four tigers' of Hong Kong, the Republic of Korea, Singapore and Taiwan, and the three newly industrializing economies (NIEs) of South East Asia: Indonesia, Malaysia and Thailand. The group had grown twice as fast as the rest of East Asia and substantially outperformed the industrial economies. The basic model incorporated in the report identifies two broad groups of policies which were crucial in delivering results. The first was the set of underlying fundamentals, such as macroeconomic stability, high investment in human capital, limited market distortions and a high degree of openness to inward foreign investment. In addition, the Gini coefficient – which measures income distribution – showed that much higher per capita income growth was accompanied by declining income inequality, and this was seen as a key issue for stable economic and social development. The second group of policies related to *selective* intervention by government in terms of industrial policy and prioritization, credit availability and government/private sector joint venturing. Underpinning both groups is the need for a developed and stable institutional structure in terms of governmental and financial infrastructures.

Islam and Chowdhry (1997) use this analysis to argue that the area can be split into three distinct groupings, namely the NIEs of Taiwan, South Korea, Hong Kong and Singapore, the ASEAN 4 of Malaysia, Indonesia, the Philippines and Thailand, and the transition economy of the People's Republic of China. The constituents of the distinctions stem from the World Bank analysis in so far as, apart from economic performance, the ASEAN 4 economies lack the technical government and expert bureaucratic management processes present in the NIEs, while generally being much richer in natural resources. Of more fundamental importance are the formal and informal relationships which are pervasive in all the economies, particularly the business/government joint venture systems, the extensive business conglomerations and the ethnic and business networks.

Human capital

The accepted impact of investment in education on economic growth has been largely in growth theory for the last 30 years. See in particular the analysis of Psacharopoulos (1994) over the years which is summed up in his survey. The analysis is also supported by other major international agencies so that, for example, the Asian Development Bank Annual Report (1996: 9) notes that the economic and social rates of return in education 'tend to be amongst the highest rates of return on all investments'. The new growth theory which has developed from the mid-1980s focuses on determinants such as investment in human capital, increasing returns to scale and the impact of openness in international trade. Sengupta (1993) undertook empirical testing of the hypotheses using NIEs in the Asia-Pacific region, notably Korea. The estimates appeared largely to support the basic theory. In particular the externality effect of human capital was seen to be an important component of the increasing returns to scale condition. Since technical progress is no longer taken as exogenous, it follows that education and training become arguments in the growth function and are the principal explanations of technical change. However, the analysis took 'on-the-job learning' as the principal investment in human capital, and of course this does not involve formal education. Hence the implications for a causal relationship between higher education (HE) and growth are not made clear by this approach.

The World Bank (1993) noted that in nearly all the rapidly growing East Asian economies the quantity and the quality of education and training had undergone significant growth and transformation. The 1995 Development in Practice series (World Bank 1995) reviewed the priorities and strategies for education and returned to the 1993 study noting that in East Asia the HPAEs showed a significantly higher rate of growth attributable to education than all the other economies.

However, and this is the key point, primary education was seen to be by far the largest single contributor to economic growth with private rates of return (enhancement of personal incomes due to education) of 39 per cent and a social rate of return (return to society at large) of 20 per cent. The comparable figures for HE were 11.7 per cent and 20 per cent. There are major problems in using this approach. Private rates are determined by the effects on individual incomes of undertaking education and are relatively easy to measure. The external or social effects are much more difficult to measure and consequently the social rate of return almost certainly understates the benefits accruing to society as a whole. Increasingly high-level technology and services – the so called 'smart' industries – involve the joint use of highly skilled human resources along with state-of-the-art technology. The more highly skilled is the labour force, the higher the level of subsequent technology. The analysis which Becker (1964) introduced is particularly appropriate to the Asian case, in that HE allows the technology transfer from other parts of the world which enables rapid growth and industrialization.

Asian values

Traditional wisdom views the countries within the Asia-Pacific region as encompassing 'Asian values'. Thus a series of conferences, workshops and seminars conducted by the Malaysian Institute of Management with sponsorship from the Konrad Adenauer Foundation in the period 1990–2 noted common underlying values of collectivism, harmony and face, loyalty and respect for authority, status, and non-assertiveness in the Malaysian workforce. On the other hand, Western values were viewed as being typified by individualism, competition, privacy, assertiveness, informality and directness. However, the reality appears to be that there is increasing congruence between the two sides with development being increasingly driven in almost all NIEs by market and capitalist forces and Western management processes by Kaizen (continuous improvement), JIT (just in time) and collective action. Consequent upon these economic shifts there have been resultant social movements. The shifting values and the encroachment of Western culture have provoked some reactive policies; for example, the increasing emphasis of the Singapore government on the learning of Mandarin and the Malaysian government's attempts, subsequently discarded, to emphasize the use of Bahasa Malaysia as the commercial and government language.

The whole region

In many ways the ASEAN region, and Malaysia and Singapore in particular, is at the crossroads of differing social and economic value systems, with considerable inward investment of resources and personnel from Japan and Korea on the one hand, and from Europe and the United States on the other. In the last few years there has been, in addition, the impact (especially for the Chinese ethnic groups) of a surging economy in the People's Republic of China. The consequence is the struggle to adopt radically differing managerial and value systems while trying to maintain an indigenous identity. Jinnosuke Miyai, president of the Japan Productivity Centre, Tokyo, observed in 1992 that 'some of the Japanese systems are so different from other advanced countries that Japanese corporations operating globally are obliged to modify their systems so as to conform with the world pattern' (Miyai 1992: 34). He also noted that the Japanese consider that the provision of required job skills is not enough in order to create an effective workforce: motivation is also necessary and the ability to be flexible and adaptable to the changing environment.

The implication is that the education system, particularly HE, needs to be able to develop an appropriate workforce to meet these requirements. To the extent that ASEAN countries adapt to Japanese experience and processes, then the role of formal education becomes less important in the development process. Recruitment of personnel is seen as an investment in long-term human assets. Specialist skills, academic standards or qualifications are less important than aptitude for business and teamwork. The skills, knowledge and aptitudes necessary for the job are seen as being developed by the organization; an approach applied also to graduate engineers, scientists and technologists on the basis that the existing knowledge base has a limited shelf-life.

The tiger miracle

The preceding analysis has identified the driving forces for the development of the ASEAN region. The Asian tiger 'miracle' is, in fact, the consequence of the congruence of the three conditions identified by Doner (1991) and the implementation of these by a combination of state/private sector interaction. Investment in human resource development has been shown to be a key argument in the production function. What started as an 'unexplained residual' with the initial studies of economic development in the 1960s has developed into the recognition of education as a key variable. Of concern in the ASEAN region is the disparity between social rates of return and private rates of return. The World Bank observed in 1990 (Haddid et al. 1990) that the gap is particularly noticeable at the HE level and that, in addition, this needs to be taken in the context of the considerably higher relative costs of such education. At the same time it recognizes that, as development occurs, the pay-off of *expanding* access to university level education is likely to be higher than expanding access to primary and secondary education.

How then should HE, at university level, 'lock in' to the development process described? The standard approach, typified by the World Bank (Haddid et al. 1990), raises more questions than it answers. There is acknowledgement that the impact of science and engineering expertise should be an engine of growth. There is the normative model of HE/training, scientific research, and the application of research outcomes and of training contributing to the production of goods and services through technological diffusion.

An ASEAN dependency model

The NIEs should be examining their research base and translating this into production processes. In this respect the role of university research and training becomes important, at least for the ability to adapt and apply external technology for the local market – the technology transfer process. It was noted above that the dependency syndrome is only part of the development process in the ASEAN region; however one of the constant macro-policy issues is the slow 'technology transfer' process. To the extent that slow transfer is a political issue, as it is in Malaysia and to a lesser extent in Singapore, then the dependency model holds. There is the common thesis that a causal link exists between the role of university scientific and technical education and economic growth. However, in many ways, what has been more important than the role of educating future recruits to that scientific-technological nexus has been the role of intermediating processes. Basically this involves the nature of the actual curriculum (knowledge versus problem solving), industry/university links at a practical level, research and development programmes in universities related to industrial needs, and the overall relationship between the universities and potential client sectors.

The World Bank admits that the evidence linking the relationships between university science and technological education as a necessary if not sufficient condition for technology transfer is 'circumstantial' (World Bank 1995: 10). Nonetheless the quantity and quality of those elements of HE are seen as strategic. This view of the impact of university education appears radically at odds with reality in Malaysia, Singapore and neighbouring countries. One of the standard arguments for increased investment in all types of education is that there is the consequence of increased equality of income: since education is a resource made available to all sectors of society it will result in a more equitable income distribution. Indeed the World Bank pursues this analysis with enthusiasm. However, as Islam and Chowdhry (1997) point out the reality is less the case. Economic growth together with increasing income equality have been seen as a significant issue in ASEAN development, and the respective Gini coefficients seem to indicate this. The title of this collection includes the term 'creation of wealth'. Perhaps the distinction between income and wealth needs to be borne in mind, and it is possible that income and redistribution of income have grown together as believed by the international agencies. However the evidence is mixed, as observed by Islam and Chowdhry.

The analysis so far has identified the key growth criteria. It is obvious that there needs to be a link between university activity and these criteria if universities are to be seen as a major change agent in the growth process. (To the extent that teacher education is undertaken by the university sector then this is a potential linkage.)

Varied functions of the university

As the World Bank (1995) notes, a university is a multiproduct firm which produces instruction, research, socialization, certification and other social functions. Evaluation of the benefits of a university is primarily undertaken via graduate earnings and employment conditions. This has severe limitations.

The link between earnings and productivity can be tenuous especially when one notes the disparity between public sector and private sector graduate salaries which has been greater in the ASEAN region than elsewhere in recent years. In Malaysia, in particular, entry to university was seen as the principal means to attaining higher-level civil service jobs. This is an example of the 'screening' view of HE whereby the award of the relevant qualification provides a market screening process for potential entrants.

In the context of the rapidly developing economies, one needs to put into place a model of how universities can be an engine of growth. There are certain features which need to be considered. Manufacturing and industrial production has been a mainstay both of total production and of exports. To date in Malaysia and Singapore this has been achieved principally by the inflow of foreign companies and capital together with technology expertise. It is noticeable that one of the major complaints of the governments and ministries of those countries has been the slow rate of technology transfer even within key sectors such as electronics and the motor industry, e.g. Proton. This is the classic version of the 'flying geese' syndrome. The same analysis applies to processing sectors such as the oil industry, although there is an increasing shift to downstream activity together with the associated technical staffing requirements. The need for skilled manpower has been essentially at the technician rather than at the research and development level. Examination of earnings by area of graduate specialization, however, reflects the fact that agriculture, engineering and science graduates all underperform in the all-subject index while medicine and economics/accountancy graduates substantially outperform the index. In addition, non-engineering and science salaries also grow faster over time. There is inevitably a time lag between the 'outputs' of universities and their impact upon the economy. Thus the full effects of any influence of university activity on growth in the 1990s needs to be stemming from that activity in the 1980s. In 1986 there were 48,000 applications in Malaysia for the 8600 university places, according to the Malaysian Ministry of Education. A similar picture emerged for Singapore. Consequently in both countries there was a steady stream of applicants who went overseas for their HE, particularly to the United Kingdom, Australia, Canada and the United States. This is a process which has been maintained in recent years but it is noticeable that, at undergraduate level, the most popular courses are in the areas of law and accountancy.

Universities and economic growth

The evidence from the earnings analyses, therefore, does not seem to indicate that the role of universities in economic growth in South East Asia has been any greater than in the advanced economies. Indeed to the extent that the expansion of the university sector has diverted funds from primary and secondary education, this may well be seen to be a substantial opportunity cost of expanding HE. This is not to say that current policy will have little effect on future growth. This can be illustrated better by the experience of the employment structure of the countries and, in particular, the demands for the various subject categories of graduates. One of the standard indicators is to take the unemployment rates and the job search rates for more than three months. Data from the 1980s shows unemployment and search rates lowest in the engineering and science areas. In the 1990s both Malaysia and Singapore have experienced full, indeed overfull, employment with very substantial inflows of migrant labour. Singapore's labour market is extremely tight with the unemployment rate at 2.6 per cent and an estimated 20 per cent of its labour force consisting of skilled and unskilled foreign workers. In Malaysia, with a similar unemployment rate of 2.9 per cent, it is estimated by the Asian Development Bank (1996) that foreign migrant workers constitute at least 0.5 million of the total labour force of 8 million. Local studies indicate a continued shortage of graduate engineers and a constant process of recruitment of expatriates to meet the gap. Both countries are at a critical point for continued development as the move from primary and from low value added, labour intensive, low skills levels to high value added, skills-based activity continues. However, the next stage is to move into the development of new products and processes on a local basis rather than to rely on existing technology transfer. It will be in this area that the impact of universities is most likely to be felt.

The services sector

Little mention has been made so far of the services sector and yet in Singapore this accounts for 60 per cent of gross domestic product (GDP). Services, particularly the financial services sector, are seen throughout the region as a major conduit for growth. The impact of HE upon this sector is at best limited – an experience common to most economies. The development of Singapore as a regional financial centre and the steady growth of the Malaysian financial markets can be attributed not to the role of universities, but to the monitoring and increased openness of the economies. Of note here is the role of foreign institutions in the training and education of managers within this sector. Universities in neither country have shown specific interest in postgraduate management education designed for working professionals. The proliferation of MBA programmes on a part-time basis has been dominated by the United Kingdom, and increasingly Australian universities from the late 1980s onwards. Indeed the size of the demand, and the willingness to pay the fees on a private basis, has, until late 1997, shown no sign of diminishing. On the basis that management education has a significant contribution to make towards the productivity and growth of an economy it is, perhaps, ironic that it is foreign universities which are providing a significant proportion of such activity. The recent currency crises, particularly for Malaysia, are having a significant impact on this trend.

This issue is part of the larger picture of the perception and status of local provision. External expertise is still seen to have kudos compared with local provision. Thus training and development programmes, provided and driven by non-local experts, attract far more support than indigenous programmes. Given the earlier comments regarding the drive to maintain 'Eastern' values, this is perhaps surprising. At the same time there is a desire and wish on the part of members of many layers of organizations to obtain qualifications the provision of which is undertaken by a variety of agencies. Thus the Singapore Institute of Management and the Malaysian Institute of Management undertake training to diploma level but also act as partners with foreign universities in the provision of postgraduate programmes. Foreign provision of programmes at both undergraduate and at postgraduate level is undertaken by private sector agencies acting as the base for a large number of distance learning programmes provided by foreign universities. At present there are more than 40 such postgraduate programmes offered in Singapore and a slightly smaller number in Malaysia. The cohorts of graduates from such programmes display an even higher degree of job mobility than the population as a whole in both countries and their earnings streams reflect the high private rates of return on investment in HE.

Private universities

There are currently ten public and four private universities in Malaysia, and two in Singapore. However, new legislation in the former is driving university structures to corporatization together with an expansion of private university provision. At the same time they are being increasingly encouraged to undertake income generation activity and to strengthen links with the private sector. It can be argued that the current links with industry in the late 1990s in Malaysia are similar to the position of universities in the United Kingdom one decade earlier, and consequently there is not a significant relationship between university activity and economic growth. That position is made even more tenable when any potential effect is subject to the time lags noted above. It has increasingly been realized that technological transfer is not a sufficient condition for development. There is also scepticism regarding a purely vocational approach to HE. The Malaysian universities have consistently adopted a United Kingdom style of university structure. This can involve dysfunctional features particularly in the status rating of subjects and knowledge. In the same way the ranking of research is still very much the 'blue skies' style referred to in Chapter 1 of this volume.

However the analysis here is complicated by government policy. Malaysia has consistently undertaken more recurrent expenditure on education than its competitor economies and yet the yield on that expenditure has been lower. In the sixth Malaysia Plan education accounted for 15 per cent of the budget (Government of Malaysia 1991). Malaysia is a multiethnic society and after the 1969 race riots the New Economic Policy of 1971 was designed to accelerate the 'trickle down' effects so that in 20 years the Bumiputra group would manage at least 30 per cent of total commercial and industrial activity. The government commenced in the 1970s to press the use of Malay as the medium of instruction in universities as a means of encouraging Bumiputra participation in HE. The university system expanded quickly in the period to 1980 with five new universities being opened. This was accompanied by a substantial expansion in government scholarships, based on need rather than merit and with informal quotas set to encourage Bumiputra numbers. The Institut Pengajian Tinggi (Institute of Advanced Studies) concluded in the early 1980s that the government was, in effect, a monopolist since almost none of the graduates coming out of the universities were absorbed into the private sector, with 90 per cent of the graduates on scholarships (two-thirds of the total student population) under bond to the government, most committed to seven years service. Pressure was felt elsewhere: in 1990 11.5 per cent of teachers were untrained. Although the objectives of the new economic policy were being met in so far as the majority of total students enrolled were Malays, there was increasing concern about a strong bias towards liberal arts and concern that the degree in itself, rather than the subject matter studied, was seen to be the principal requirement for government employment. Parallel to these developments was the growth of overseas HE, so that by 1987 there were 65,000 students in the tertiary sector in Malaysia and 40,000 studying overseas.

Universities and economic change

Given the lagged function pointed out above in the ASEAN dependency model, economic development in Malaysia from the mid-1980s onwards should have been affected by university developments from the mid-1970s. There were certainly major developments occurring in the university sector but the purposes were social rather than economic, attempting to engineer a shift of access initially and hence a shift in the economic balance of the principal ethnic groups. Psacharopoulus (1980) describes Malaysian universities as a 'failed change agent', citing studies which argue inappropriate transfer of planning models from the West, meaningless syllabus distinctions, and lack of university participation in government research or in consultancy. The consultancy on the Klang Valley development project, which has been one of the principal regional engines of manufacturing growth, was turned down by the University of Malaya on the basis of lack of sufficient managerial and technical skills.

Small and medium sized enterprises (SMEs) have been an important element of the growth process in most of the ASEAN region. A recent unpublished survey undertaken by the University of Hull on the Klang Valley noted the relatively low level of educational attainment of both workers and entrepreneurs. Although SMEs act as both feeders to large scale enterprises and as a strong element in their own right, the impact of the tertiary sector upon them has been minimal. Once again job training and specialist courses have been the principal means of training and development. The picture however is different in Singapore where the level of educational attainment in SMEs is considerably higher. At the other end of the spectrum the Singapore bureaucracy is staffed with high status, highly skilled technocrats and managers. The close links between government agencies, statutory boards, ministries and the private sector – notably the 'government linked corporations' – have resulted in the analysis of the country as being predominantly a corporate state. A considerable part of the growth process has been driven by the re-export sector and the openness of the economy as reflected in its very high international trade/GDP ratio. Singapore's universities have followed the traditional path of academic excellence and evaluation of research on peer-group assessment. Early government emphasis on electronics and associated industries as the economy moved to a high value added base was reflected in the complementary emphasis on engineering and technology within the entire education system. Although there are considerable elements both of students studying overseas and of foreign universities running programmes within Singapore itself, the balance is considerably less distorted than in the case of Malaysia. Labour shortages in Singapore have resulted in the implementation of training programmes for older workers as a key initiative in relieving pressure, and the adult education department at the National University of Singapore has been instrumental in this process.

Conclusion: the role of formal education

What conclusions follow from this analysis? Of course each Asian tiger economy is different but there are common features which have been noted above. The close relationship of government and industry, networking in various forms and openness to the international economy have been driving forces. While low absolute wages are a possible condition, what is far more important is low wage costs – i.e. money wages relative to labour productivity. Labour productivity in turn depends upon the capital/labour ratio and the knowledge, skills and abilities of the entire labour force. Formal education plays a substantive role in the attainment of knowledge and skills. However the shelf-life of such elements is becoming increasingly short and the 'learning by doing' emphasis has been a strong element of increasing labour productivity in the ASEAN region. Universities in that region still tend to be relatively élitist and there is no current expectation of access to mass HE. The consequence is a surfeit of motivated, qualified applicants for restricted places and a consequent spillover to foreign institutions both domestically and overseas. University education is seen as an access mode to the higher reaches of the private and public sector. The latter is particularly well illustrated in the context of Singapore with its strong corporate government approach.

The implication is that the experience of the rapidly growing economies does not provide a role model for the future development of universities in the developed world (bearing in mind that Singapore now has a higher gross national product (GNP) per head than the United Kingdom). If anything the causal link has been the reverse; namely that rapid economic development has allowed the universities to develop rather than vice versa. The ability to sustain recent growth rates came under severe pressure in the late part of 1997. Thailand, Malaysia, Indonesia and South Korea have all suffered substantial pressure on their exchange rates and a radical downward revision of their future potential. This is an issue of underlying fundamentals, not merely a response to financial 'blips' and is a strong indicator of the importance of the underlying precondition for growth noted above. Indeed links between the university sector and the major determinants of growth are stronger in the United Kingdom than in the countries discussed above. Chapter 1 notes that establishment of many universities is a response to industrial and trade needs. Prior to independence the same cannot be claimed of the universities set up in the ASEAN region. Consequent upon independence, with the expansion of the university sector, the perceived needs tended to be in the professions rather than in technology. The same holds largely true today. To the extent that the experience of university education encourages the ability to think, adopt and adapt, then these are universal objectives. The fact that curriculum structure and educational processes are similar in the United Kingdom and the fast growing economies suggests more about the universality of university processes than about universities being a significant explanatory variable in fast growing economies.

References

Akamatsu, K. (1960) A theory of balanced growth in the world economy. *Weltwirtschaftliches Archiv*, 86(2), 17–23.
Asian Development Bank (1996) *Annual Report*. Manila, Asian Development Bank.
Asma, A. (ed.) (1992) *Understanding the Malaysian Workforce*. Kuala Lumpur, Malaysian Institute of Management.
Becker, G.S. (1964) *Human Capital: A Theoretical and Empirical Analysis with Special Reference to Education* (General Series 30). New York, Columbia University Press.
Behrman, J.R. (1990) *Human Resource Led Development*. New Delhi, ILO-ARTEP
Doner, R.F. (1991) Approaches to the politics of economic growth in South East Asia. *Journal of Asian Studies*, 50(4), 818–49.
Government of Malaysia (1991) *Malaysia Plan*. Kuala Lumpur, Government Printer.
Haddid, B. *et al.* (1990) *Education and Development – Evidence for New Priorities*. Washington DC, World Bank.
Islam, I. and Chowdhry, A. (1997) *Asia-Pacific Economics: A Survey*. London, Routledge.
Klitgaard, R. (1991) *Adjusting to Reality: Beyond the State Versus Market in Economic Development*. San Francisco, ICS Press.
Miyai, J. (1992) The Japanese approach to human resource development. *International Productivity Journal*, II, reprinted in the *Productivity Digest*, November.

Psacharopoulos, G. (1980) *Higher Education in Developing Countries*. Washington DC, World Bank.

Psacharopoulos, G. (1994) Return to investment in education: a global update. *World Development*, v (22).

Psacharopoulos, G. and Woodhall, M. (1985) *Education for Development: An Analysis of Investment Choices*. New York, Oxford University Press.

Salleh, I.M. and Meyanathan, S.D. (1993) *The Lessons of East Asia: Malaysia*. Washington DC, World Bank.

Sengupta, J.K. (1993) Growth in NICs in Asia: some tests of new growth theory. *Journal of Development Studies*, 29(2), 342–57.

Soon, T.W. and Tan, C.S. (1993) *The Lessons of East Asia: Singapore*. Washington DC, World Bank.

Thant, M., Tang, M. and Kakazu, H. (eds) (1994) *Growth Triangles in Asia*. Hong Kong, Asian Development Bank, Oxford University Press.

World Bank (1993) *The East Asian Miracle*. New York, Oxford University Press.

World Bank (1995) *Priorities and Strategies for Education: A World Bank Review*. Washington DC, World Bank.

Part 2

Examples and Cases

Introduction

Universities are almost impenetrable organizations. Although it is usual to speak of them as if they were conventional corporate bodies, they are not so. Universities are places where individual academics pursue what are for the most part individual careers located in personal academic networks. This is one of the key reasons why universities are virtually impossible to manage, and it is not much use trying to think of them as homogenous entities.

The conventional wisdom suggests that the new universities (that is, the former polytechnics) are more corporate than the older ones, but this in fact is not the case. Corporateness in university terms is a consequence of traditional practice and a long period of accommodation to the varying interests that vie for resources. Universities cannot be managed or brought into coherence by fiat, only by practical internal cooperation.

This is exactly what the following cases show. It is the process of an institution's development as the sum of its parts that is critical to corporate activity. The origins usually arise from some sort of crisis and opportunist remedy. Such crises are usually not publicly advertised and one has either to know the truth from experience or read between the lines. It seems that universities only respond to threats from outside – internal threats only disturb the comfort of daily living – and then there has to be some leadership (generally 'from the top') to turn challenge into opportunity.

And history certainly counts. There are few surprises in the history of universities especially as only three of them (Oxford, Cambridge and Durham) do not have some kind of previous economic purpose in their foundation, usually a college of commerce, arts and manufacturing. English universities should take naturally to economic opportunity, and the idea that they are lost in a dream world of academe does not stand up to much scrutiny.

It is possible therefore to identify some long trends of economic awareness and involvement that augur well for future adaptability. Some departments resolutely keep to their historical task of doing applied research and teaching in spite of pressure from the funding bodies to compete in the research and teaching assessment exercises as rarefied bodies. When universities receive official encouragement backed by resources from the government, many of them will be in a strong position to change their modes of operation within a strongly established character of being on the best of terms with business, industry and the public services.

7

Universities and Communities: Cases from North-East England

Derek Fraser

One of the undeniable constraints in developing regional activities in support of local communities has been the variability of regional identity. The sense of identity within a defined geographical or political entity has been perceptibly greater in some regions of the UK than in others. However as the *Dearing Report* confirmed, in the North-East 'the long history of regional thinking and working means that there is a willingness on the part of stakeholders to form alliances'.[1] No better example illustrates this point than HESIN (Higher Education Support for Industry in the North), formed by the North-Eastern universities, and the Knowledge House initiative which grew from it. Within a region where there is an explicit desire to promote inward investment, collaboration and partnership, the three post-1992 universities have developed distinctive activities aimed at community benefit. This chapter explores the varying ways in which the 'modern universities' of the North-East have defined and implemented a community role.

Teesside

The University of Teesside began life in 1929/30 as Constantine College. Middlesbrough had grown rapidly on the banks of the Tees during the nineteenth century on the strength of coal, iron, engineering and shipbuilding. What Gladstone called 'the infant Hercules' outstripped in importance its more historic neighbours, Stockton and Hartlepool, and became the sub-regional capital of Teesside.[2] The town's education and training provision lagged well behind the need for a skilled labour force. To remedy this deficiency, shipbuilder Joseph Constantine donated £40,000 in the late 1920s to establish a college for advanced technical training which would meet the needs of local industry.[3]

Constantine College built a fine local reputation, particularly for part-time advanced technical training and, after four decades of successful development, was one of the first group of institutions to be designated as a polytechnic. Though the creation of the polytechnic was recognition both for the town and the region, there was some disappointment that Teesside did not have its own university. As local supporters pointed out, in 1964 Teesside's 600,000 was 'the largest centre of population in the country without a university', and two years later the promoters argued that 'the case for the Technological University of Teesside is not quantitative but qualitative'.[4] Eventually, and perhaps unexpectedly, Teesside got its university in 1992, somewhat unaware that since 1970 it had had a university in all but name.

Given that its origins and history had been so much rooted in its community, the University of Teesside found a natural developmental role as a community university. Positioning itself as 'the opportunity university', Teesside committed itself to 'provide a particular focus for the development of the educational, cultural, social and economic life of the community' (mission statement). With about a third of its students from the Teesside area, within the two-thirds from the North-East, the university has promoted access and participation within its natural hinterland. In this respect the university has adopted some of the characteristics of the so-called 'metropolitan universities' of the USA described by Ernest Lynton:

> A metropolitan university's regional orientation and strong commitment to serve the intellectual needs of its surrounding communities and constituencies, the resulting diversity of the student body, the focus on the education of practitioners and the emphasis on outreach through applied research and technical assistance....[5]

The University of Teesside Partnership, comprising the university and its nine associated further education (EE) colleges, has created a regional ladder of opportunity, facilitating progression at the interface between FE and higher education (HE). The university, with the support of the Higher Education Funding Council for England (HEFCE), has established a summer college aimed at non-traditional students and has extended the college's lifelong learning programme to local companies such as Samsung at Wynyard. The university's Centre for Community Education conducts outreach work among disadvantaged social groups, such as the unemployed and ethnic minority communities, offering both vocational programmes of study and business advice. The University of Teesside was the first university to host and deliver the Prince's Trust development programme, aimed mainly at local unemployed young people.

These examples provide some insight into the university's broader social and economic role and there are specific initiatives which illustrate this further. The university has established the Community Informatics Research Applications Unit (CIRA), whose role is to utilize informatics to take learning opportunities into the community.

We are living through an 'information revolution', as profound as the industrial revolution of the late eighteenth century. There has been an explosion of information which, on some estimates, now leads to a doubling of knowledge every decade or so. Simultaneously, there has been a revolution in connectivity which allows real-time access to this information. These changes will undoubtedly influence the way people access knowledge and learn from it. CIRA seeks both to deliver learning opportunities through the new technology and to conduct research so that we may understand better the impact of this new technology upon communities.

In officially launching CIRA at the university in 1996, Tony Blair (then leader of the opposition) drew attention to the potential danger of the new technology: 'Like the University of Teesside, I don't want to see inequality in the information age. It is vital we narrow any gaps between the information rich, with access to computers and the Internet, and the information poor who, at the moment, lack access to the Information Society'.[6] It is to address this danger specifically that CIRA has established university outposts in the community, with the equipment and training necessary to utilize the new technology.

No doubt because it is in the prime minister's constituency, the best known example of this initiative is the Trimdon 2000 project. Here the university is working with this south-Durham village in its attempt to revitalize and regenerate a former mining community. The university has provided computers in the local community college, the library and the Labour Club, and British Telecom has provided on-line access to the Internet. CIRA has delivered the training and advice, particularly aimed at building confidence in the use of the new technology. From within their own community, Trimdon village residents can obtain university certificates, as well as participate in the Trimdon 2000 initiative. In 1997 the prime minister switched on Trimdon as a model digital village with its own website, the result of a very special partnership between a university and a village community. CIRA has other sites in deprived areas of Middlesbrough, Ayresome and Hemlington, and has been commissioned to develop a coherent information strategy for the whole of Teesside. CIRA is one example of community involvement, and the regional industrial community is the context for a second case study.

In the Western world, universities have found it far from straightforward to respond to the needs of industry. Much government rhetoric, such as the White Paper *Realising Our Potential* (1993) or the Technology Foresight exercise, extols the importance of the symbiotic relationship between universities and industry. Yet, in practice, the mutual imperatives of responding to industrially-defined technical, research or training needs and delivering mainstream core teaching and research have often proved difficult to coalesce. The problem is often one of focus, on both sides. To quote Lynton again, 'to fulfil its external mission with optimal effectiveness, a university must work with its constituencies and clients in defining problems and issues, identifying pertinent factors and developing appropriate approaches'.[7]

It was just this approach which led the University of Teesside to establish The European Process Industries Competitiveness Centre (EPICC). During the recession of the early 1980s, Teesside witnessed some dramatic structural changes in the local economy which saw the demise of some famous local companies and the decline of traditional industries. This was well encapsulated in the famously staged 1987 walkabout by Prime Minister Margaret Thatcher on a derelict site by the Tees, where formerly had stood the well-known engineering firm of Head Wrightson. That whole area has subsequently been radically redesigned and redeveloped by the Teesside Development Corporation. At the same time the companies which did survive downsized and outsourced some of what were seen as non-core functions in the relentless pressure to cut costs.

By the early 1990s there was a growing concern both on Teesside and beyond that these developments were having deleterious effects. The idea of EPICC essentially grew out of three strands of contemporary development. Locally, there was a sense of loss of expertise, as much research and development (R&D) and advanced training capacity had been eroded. Nationally, there were the Competitiveness White Papers which identified strong international competitive pressures, particularly from the Far East, and which led to Michael Heseltine's various innovation initiatives at the Department of Trade and Industry (DTI). Third, the European Community (EC) was promoting inter-company initiatives to develop and share expertise among market leading manufacturers across Europe.

There were senior industrialists on Teesside who were personally familiar with all three developments and from them, and from the conversations between them and the university, emerged the concept of a centre of expertise dedicated to the process industries, rather like the Warwick Manufacturing Centre's early connection with the motor industry.[8] The idea of the centre gained local industrial support and a project team of secondees from the private and public sectors was housed in the university to develop the idea further. Under the aegis of Teesside Tomorrow, a local business support alliance, the partners' steering group of the early initiative successfully bid for significant funding from the Single Regeneration Budget (SRB). In December 1994, the minister for Teesside, Baroness Blatch, visited the university to announce that £1.3 million had been granted to the embryonic EPICC over a seven-year period. This funding was further enhanced by successful bids for European Regional Development Fund (ERDF) grants.

So, the immediate future for this initiative was secure, and so far the university's role had been to assist in the articulation of the concept, to create and facilitate the partnerships and to provide the necessary academic credibility for the project. From the first it was agreed that EPICC must be industry-led and responsive to industrial needs. This was not simply the case of the university making its expertise available to industry on a shop-window basis, as had often been the case. Given the provenance of EPICC, the ideal vehicle for taking the project forward was a joint venture company between the four main sponsors, ICI, British Steel, Teesside Training and Enterprise Council (TEC) and the university. However, legal difficulties together with strategic policy decisions by the companies meant that the first preference could not be adopted. Indeed it might be said that in the event, it was only the university that had the capability and willingness to underwrite the project. The board of governors agreed in 1995, not without some understandable worries about potential liabilities, to establish EPICC as a wholly owned subsidiary company.

However, in conformity with the conceptual framework of the key strategic objective, EPICC was not intended to be a university company of the traditional sort. Only one university member, the vice-chancellor, sits on the board, which is comprised of leading industrialists from ICI, Zeneca, British Steel and Northumbrian Water, together with the chief executive of the Tees Valley Development Company and the president of the German Fraunhofer Society. EPICC's chief executive, Dr Ray Sheahan, is a former senior manager with Zeneca and the company has recruited a small core staff from the senior ranks of industry, government and academia. EPICC has attracted support and encouragement from Government Office North East as part of the Three Rivers regional strategy, with parallel and complementary centres on the Tees, Tyne and Wear.

EPICC identified its role as an independent industry-led organization which could broker a number of key areas of support. These included:

- Company and management restructuring to produce flatter, leaner organizations focused on core activities.
- Innovative training packages to foster a culture of continuous improvement through the development of people.
- Developing a cooperative rather than adversarial approach to supply chain management and increasing the scope for high quality outsourcing.
- Rationalization of technical resources, their ownership and availability.
- Cross-company collaborations on R&D technology transfer and the identification and adopting of best practice.
- Championing recognized routes to improved competitiveness.

The first challenge for EPICC was to develop a range of products and services which were aligned with these industry requirements. The second challenge was to do this in a way which bridged the worlds of industry and academia. EPICC services and products are being developed in three areas: people and organizational development; research and technology development; and industrial services and networking.

In the areas of education and training EPICC's products and services include:

- A substantial programme of seminars specifically designed for the process industries and backed by case studies delivered by companies.
- A unique ten-module M.Sc. in process manufacturing management, validated and accredited by the University of Teesside.

This Teesside M.Sc. provides understanding of and training in the skills required to manage all aspects of manufacturing in the process industries. The course is available both full- and part-time and a significant part of the teaching is delivered by leading experts from industry which provides a strong sense of relevance. Indeed the course was developed by a team of people from both the university and industry.

EPICC has also developed an innovative and demanding programme through which companies learn about improving competitiveness by visiting each other, and has organized conferences relevant to the process industries. A broader role for EPICC is to work with groups of companies, identifying their joint training needs, and then providing coordinated access to available training capability both inside and outside of EPICC. Accessing funding on behalf of industry to develop innovative training courses has also been an activity for EPICC.

In the area of R&D, EPICC's role is to identify R&D themes with potential for improving the competitiveness of the process industries. This requires that the real needs of industry are understood through a whole series of techniques – including focus groups which have proved to be excellent vehicles for identifying R&D themes generic to the process industries. EPICC links these requirements with groups in various universities and other institutions which have research capability and puts together proposals and bids for funds on a regional, national and European basis. The funding bodies see the benefits of having EPICC as an honest broker and intelligent interpreter of industry requirements. As a consequence EPICC's success rate at accessing R&D and training funding for industry and academia has been substantially higher than the norm. A substantial role for EPICC is to complement the fundamental work which is done by academics, by converting those ideas into forms which can more readily be taken on by industry.

A key networking role for EPICC is to stimulate collaboration between companies in non-competitive areas and provide various ways for companies to share best practices. One way in which this is brought about is through focus groups, typically composed of 10–15 companies complemented where appropriate by experts from universities. These groups identify the key areas affecting competitiveness and develop activities to fill gaps and bring about improvements. These may be training requirements, R&D projects or services that companies require. One example of accessing support facilities and expertise not available to companies elsewhere has been the creation by EPICC of a pilot plant brokerage service for the UK chemical industry. Other initiatives include facilitating the outsourcing of an activity, which has not been done particularly well by companies. EPICC also offers a benchmarking service using a range of tools available to the company.

Some of the areas covered by focus groups include:

- people and organization development;
- process control;
- environment/clean technologies;
- benchmarking;
- management of R&D;
- manufacturing reliability.

The overall capabilities which EPICC is developing are based on a growing knowledge of the factors affecting the competitiveness of the process industries and the issues which need to be addressed. This is coupled with a growing capability to assemble a range of existing products and services to meet industry's requirements or developing new ones if they do not exist.

Since EPICC has been designed as a company outside the normal mould for university companies, it is not surprising that there have been a few difficulties in developing its distinctive role. In some cases, EPICC needs to promote and sell itself as quite distinct from the university, while in others its success is necessarily bound inextricably to that of the university. That is not an easy relationship to maintain, since there is ample potential for confusing and ambiguous messages to be received both by industry and by the academic community. Academics whose core primary role lies in EPICC nevertheless need to maintain their academic lifeblood from within the university. Moreover, as with all industrially-related research and consultancy, the rhythms, culture and contractual arrangements of academia have to be tempered and moderated to respond to industrial business practice and timescales.

Notwithstanding these important challenges, EPICC is developing successfully, and undoubtedly the seed-bed from which that success has grown was the close relationship between the University of Teesside and its industrial and business community. Because of this, there were good lines of communication with industrial leaders, a sensitivity to changing business needs, a capacity to respond imaginatively as opportunities arose and the academic expertise in specifically relevant areas. In this context EPICC is a distinctive and specially structured variant of the 'open for business' approach the university has adopted. This philosophy underpins the initiative which all the universities in the North-East have joined: Knowledge House.

Through Knowledge House's single phone number, small and medium sized enterprises can access the expertise of the region's universities. Many companies are largely unaware of the potential of universities as sources of advice and business support. Examples of the way the University of Teesside responded to Knowledge House enquiries illustrate how the scheme is working. In one case, the university was able to provide a stress analysis expert to develop a PC-based system to calculate the stress levels within its onsite pipeline repairs enclosure. In another, a cycle tyre company is working with the university on increasing the visibility of cyclists by incorporating fibre optics into tyres. In a third case, a firm in the North-East won a contract to work on the largest solar-powered building in the UK, following advice from the university, which, according to the firm, showed an impressive commercial understanding.[9]

Finally, the university has been able to assist a fibreglass company by conducting confirmatory tests on rigid polyurethane closed-cell foam. The production manager of this company revealed that he had never used a university before and was unsure of what to expect, 'but I have to say I was very impressed with the rapid response . . . I would recommend any company with a technical problem to consider using Knowledge House'.[10] It was no doubt testimony such as this which convinced the Dearing Committee to give such a ringing endorsement of Knowledge House, to advocate its adoption nationally:

> Many institutions across the UK have taken initiatives to build bridges, but the problem for institutions and small and medium sized enterprises is great. We suggest that there may be advantage in building on the initiatives already taking place, through the creation of a national **Knowledge House**, operated at local and regional levels. This would enable small firms to access a port of inquiry in their local higher education institutions, by using one national telephone number.[11]

In this significant respect this pioneering North-Eastern experience is deemed to have national application.[12]

Northumbria

The University of Northumbria at Newcastle is, of course, a player within Knowledge House and indeed one of the early successes was the university's design expertise, which solved the problem of pattern making for a fledgling manufacturer of children's nursery furniture. Northumbria has also pioneered effective collaboration with the TECs and this university's activity and experiences with Tyneside TEC were featured as a case study in a recent important national survey.[13] Furthermore, Northumbria academics have done extensive work on the impact of their university on the local economy. For example, they estimated that in 1992/3, the activities of the University of Northumbria accounted for around £120m of expenditure and some 5000 full-time equivalent (fte) jobs.[14] These academics have recently extended their studies to catalogue and evaluate in both quantitative and qualitative terms the extensive range of linkages which bind the university to its community. It is a model study which merits emulation across the university system.[15]

Northumbria has an explicit commitment to its wider region, including, but also beyond, the city of Newcastle. A good example of this is the collaboration with Northumberland TEC in establishing a management centre at Longhirst Hall, near Morpeth. The Northumberland TEC area lacked an HE facility and as part of a joint initiative, the TEC purchased the building with the support of European Social Fund (ESF) and ERDF funding. The TEC rents the site to the university, which provides national and international business programmes at postgraduate, undergraduate and diploma levels. Management skills training is also provided for local industry, commerce and the public services. An even bigger enterprise which exemplifies the university's outreach commitment to its wider region is the establishment of the Carlisle campus.[16]

Carlisle is, of course, some distance from Newcastle, but there are historical and geographical links which bind the extreme north-west of England with the extreme North-East. Historically, Carlisle had been the westernmost outpost of the ancient kingdom of Northumbria. Patterns of trade and movement of population had traditionally been as much on an east/west axis in this part of England as north/south. Moreover, in the overarching government regional arrangements, Cumbria has been considered to be part of the northern region which comprises the rest of the North-East of England. The BBC also considers Carlisle to be in the North-East. So the Carlisle campus of the University of Northumbria is not so much a remote access facility as an exemplification of a wider regional commitment, a responsibility which is very explicit in the university's mission.

Rather like the citizens of Teesside, those of Carlisle were disappointed that they did not gain a university during the expansion of the 1960s. In the wake of the Robbins Report of 1963, there was indeed a decision to create a university in the far north-west, but this was in the event sited at Lancaster not Carlisle. The county of Cumbria was not thereafter well provided with HE places and, for example, in 1992/3 only 3 per cent of awards for HE made by Cumbria County Council were for places within the county boundary. In addition to this concern over the lack of HE places in the county as a whole, there were specific concerns which the historic city of Carlisle was expressing. A project known as Carlisle 2000 identified the lack of HE facilities within the city as a negative feature. The city itself took the initiative in seeking partner universities to develop an HE provision within the city. This initiative was strongly backed by local business and commerce and the local MP.

What the city of Carlisle needed was not simply a distant university with an imperialist tendency, but a university that had a genuine commitment to increasing regional participation and a sense of responsibility for the economic and social well-being of the north of England. The University of Northumbria at Newcastle was the chosen partner within the Carlisle 2000 initiative and the campus was created and opened for business in 1992. Whereas in Teesside the joint initiative between the Universities of Durham and Teesside developed University College Stockton on a redeveloped site with brand-new buildings, the university campus at Carlisle was to utilize existing historic buildings. The city council owned some historic buildings at the centre of the city and these were chosen as the site for the new university campus. It proved a major architectural and construction challenge to adapt historic buildings, most of which were grade two listed, to the needs of a modern learning environment. An eighteenth-century tea warehouse and an old brewery were the main components of an imaginative refurbishment and adaptation project which in 1995 won a British Urban Regeneration Association Award. The project combined the historic past with the needs of modern education and training, successfully integrating the restoration of historic buildings with the provision of up-to-date educational technology. As two of those who now work in Carlisle describe it:

The conversion managed to retain many of the original features of the buildings (cornices, friezes, fireplaces and staircases) at the same time as providing modern features such as interconnecting walkways, ornamental gates and ironwork, and commissioned artworks to form part of the fabric of the building. Two separate clusters of buildings are joined by an ornamental garden open to the public ... The result of the conversion and restoration works has created an environment which is pleasing to work in for both students and staff, and which is visually and aesthetically attractive.[17]

An equally successful conversion took place some small distance from the main campus with the use of a disused brewery which was originally built in 1756, but had long fallen into disuse and disrepair. The acquisition of a residence facility enabled the campus not only to meet the needs of students, but also to create opportunities for income generation from vacation conferences and other activities. In all, some £7 million has been invested by both the city council and the university to establish and develop the Carlisle campus.

The University of Northumbria estimates that in 1994/5 the staff and students of the Carlisle campus contributed nearly £3 million to the city's economy. In the following year there were some 800 students in Carlisle and over 30 staff, all of whom were filling new posts in the local labour market. The staff represent a significant addition to the pool of expertise available locally and have become involved in local initiatives such as the Carlisle City-Centre Customer Charter project and the Carlisle Campus Business Barometer. Moreover, the influx of talented well-qualified young people to university courses has helped to offset the net outflow of the young from the Carlisle area and has therefore created a more balanced social mix within the city. The refurbishments have enhanced the city's attraction as a tourist centre and themselves are a major factor in urban regeneration. The Carlisle campus thus represents an important example of the mutual benefits which may be derived from dynamic partnership between a university and its regional community.

Sunderland

The University of Sunderland in one important respect is at the very centre of the North-East HE collaboration. Most of the initiatives are in fact housed in new university buildings, which have been developed as part of the Wear riverside regeneration. HESIN, Knowledge House, the Regional Technology Centre and the recently-established Northern Business Forum all have their headquarters at Sunderland University. As with Northumbria, Sunderland has sought to quantify its impact on the local economy. The university estimates that it contributes nearly £100 million of expenditure which generates around 2500 fte jobs and that its annual output of graduates who remain in the city contributes a further £13 million.[18]

The most obvious exemplification of the university's integration within its community is its important role within the City of Sunderland Partnership, which has the aim of 'Regenerating Britain's Newest City'. The partnership brings together the local authority, chamber of commerce, development corporation, TEC and the university. It is clear that the university's role and activities are critical to the success of many of the objectives of the partnership. One of those concerns the environment, and the university has launched an environmental initiative called USER (University of Sunderland Environmental Report). This monitors and judges the university's commitment to environmental responsibility and is part of the university aim to 'encourage through links with the community the promotion of environmental responsibility and environmental protection by relevant external individuals, groups and organisations.'[19] There are two further examples which are discussed next at greater length: the Industry Centre and Learning World.

In 1990 the university established the Industry Centre, as a user-friendly, proactive, 'one-stop shop'. It aims to play a leading role in local economic development and regeneration through upgrading skills, encouraging innovation, supporting inward investment and indigenous business start-ups, and helping companies address the challenges and opportunities of their markets. The most striking aspects of the Centre are the innovative ways in which it works in close cooperation with partners to make a real impact on the local economy – from playing a key role in attracting multinational, high-tech inward investment to providing support for smaller companies where 'technology transfer' must be directly relevant to real business needs, and be practical rather than 'leading edge'.

In an area that has suffered the demise of its traditional industries, the university has been successful in developing effective, innovative and sustainable approaches to industrial regeneration across a wide range of disciplines – from the introduction of information technology (IT) in 150 small companies to the establishment of a regional centre of excellence for the high-volume and automotive manufacturing sector, from local supplier development to incubation for new business start-ups, from high-tech rapid prototyping to awareness-raising for the information society.

The Industry Centre is a model approach to the involvement of HE institutions in local and regional economic regeneration and development. It has shown how a university can be the 'motor', injecting new impetus, dynamism and innovation into an area struggling to find a new economic base. Acting alone and in partnership it is making a significant contribution to the regeneration of the region. Its structures and approaches have led the way in the region and are now serving as exemplars for other regions and nations in terms of their presentation, organization and resourcing.

Through the Industry Centre, local industry employers and the professions can access the university's expertise in addressing real business problems and challenges. The Centre presents its capacity in terms of a 'multidisciplined business development resource' which can offer solutions in the areas of:

- health care, particularly in pharmaceuticals and health sciences;
- communications, such as language provision, including Japanese;
- creativity, with specialisms in glass and media;
- education, including vocational and work-based programmes;
- IT, utilizing the MTC consultancy founded in 1984;
- business, with emphasis upon human resources, quality and supply chain;
- environment, providing the capability of ESAS, an environmental consultancy;
- manufacturing, specializing in advanced manufacturing systems.

So Sunderland University's Industry Centre established itself as a gateway into the university, adopting an approach that was later to be used by both Business Link and Knowledge House.[20]

Learning World utilizes an even more radical approach to accessing and delivering learning. Learning World is a joint initiative of the University of Sunderland and Gateshead College, and quite literally takes learning opportunities out into society. Learning World is located at the Gateshead MetroCentre, one of the largest retail parks in Europe. Learning World's potential customers are the 6000 employees who work at the MetroCentre and the 26 million shoppers and visitors who enjoy its facilities each year. Visitors to the MetroCentre daily equal the population of a town the size of Oxford: many come not to shop, but to visit the ten-screen cinema, play quasar laser or go bowling. Beyond the MetroCentre itself are the 100,000 households within 20 minutes' travel, including West Gateshead, who have no other FE or HE facility; and very importantly the 8000 employees who work at the neighbouring Team Valley industrial estate.

Learning World has developed a learning environment appropriate to its retail setting and the courses are based upon customer needs. The courses are flexibly delivered to match college or university awards. Through electronic means students can access the facilities of the college, the university and beyond. The combination of long opening times and location is attractive to many people who cannot or do not wish to attend a more traditional educational establishment. There are multiple starting and exit points for the programmes of study. Employees who work at the MetroCentre or nearby find Learning World an easy and accessible opportunity to learn with a minimum of time away from the workplace.

The initiative, which is summed up by the slogan 'It's all under one roof at Learning World' has proved attractive and innovative. Nearly 2000 students and over 300 companies have accessed the facilities in the first year, exceeding the expected targets.[21]

Conclusion

In these varying ways, the modern universities of the North-East illustrate how universities can interface with their local and regional communities in mutually enhancing ways. Of course, these universities also deliver the traditional core activities of teaching and research, and on a large scale. All three are by historic standards big universities, each graduating between 3000 and 5000 newly-qualified students each year. In terms of income and mainstream activity, providing for the needs of tens of thousands of full- and part-time students is naturally the core business. But there is no sense in which these three universities see their community and regional role as peripheral or incidental. Rather, it is at the very heart of how they define a modern university.

Indeed the examples discussed in this chapter all have interactive effects upon the core activities in a mutually reinforcing causal relationship. In summary, there is a rich diversity of activity:

At Teesside	• Using 'the opportunity university' to enhance access.
• Utilizing informatics to create community learning opportunities.
• Establishing EPICC as a vehicle for improved regional competitiveness.
At Northumbria	• Working imaginatively and productively with the TECs.
• Creating a new university campus in Carlisle.
At Sunderland	• Providing the city with a one-stop shop Industry Centre.
• Taking education to the people through Learning World.

These are but a selection of initiatives and enterprises which demonstrate how the Further and Higher Education Act (1992) broadened the definition of a university to encompass the polytechnic tradition. The polytechnics were, in effect, the community universities of their day and these modern universities are refashioning and redeveloping their community role in ways relevant to our contemporary society.

Notes and references

1. NCIHE (National Committee of Enquiry into Higher Education) (1997) *Higher Education in the Learning Society* (the Dearing Report), Report 9 'Higher Education in the Regions', para 5.5, p. 178.
2. For the history of Middlesbrough see A.J. Pollard (ed.) (1996) *Middlesbrough Town & Community 1830–1950*, Stroud, Sutton.
3. See J.W. Leonard, *Constantine College*, Teesside Polytechnic, 1981.
4. 'Proposal for the Location of a New Special Institution for Scientific and Technological education and research on Tees-side' (September 1964, unpublished). 'A Plan for the New Technological University of Tees-side' (March 1966, unpublished).
5. Ernest A. Lynton (1993) 'What is a metropolitan university?', *The Maine Scholar*, 6, 94. For a fuller discussion see D.M. Johnson and D.A. Bell (eds) (1995) *Metropolitan Universities*, Dallas, University of Texas Press.

108   *Derek Fraser*

6. Quoted in *Universe*, 25, October 1996, p. 1.
7. Ernest A. Lynton, op. cit.
8. The process industries are defined as those which change the physical or chemical state of materials. The sector includes food, pharmaceuticals, biotechnology, chemicals, utilities and metal production. It is estimated that the majority of the UK process industry capacity is within a 60-mile radius of Teesside.
9. See press reports in *Financial Times*, 11 March 1997; *Mail on Sunday*, 27 July 1997.
10. *Managing Change*, Autumn 1996, 19.
11. NCIHE, op. cit. para. 12.49, p. 199.
12. That the North-East experience is not generally replicated elsewhere is illustrated in a report on Central London which concluded 'London businesses and the public sector industries do not make extensive use of the HEIs' technical and human resources, probably because they are unaware of their extent' HEFCE (Higher Education Funding Council for England) (1997) *Higher Education and the London Economy: a Study of Linkages*, London, Focus Central, March 1997.
13. HEFCE (Higher Education Funding Council for England/DfEE (Department for Education and Employment) (1997) *Best Practice in Collaboration between Higher Education Institutions and Training & Enterprise Councils*, Bristol, HEFCE/DfEE, pp. 49–53.
14. I. Lincoln, I. Stone and A. Walker (1995) The contribution of Newcastle's higher education sector to the local economy: income and employment effects, *Northern Economic Review*, 24, 19–24. For a review of the methodology on impact studies see I.D. Duff and B. Suthers (1995) *Employment and Income Generation Effects of Institutes of Higher Education: The Town & Gown Interface, Teesside*, Teesside Business School, Monograph GEN 23.
15. Northern Economic Research Unit (1997) *Local Impact of the University of Northumbria: A Study Based on an Audit of University-Community Linkages*, University of Northumbria at Newcastle.
16. The ensuing text is based upon an undated, unpublished paper, 'The impact of a university campus upon urban economic regeneration', by D.W.G. Hind and R. Smith. I am grateful to Professor Robin Smith for allowing me to cite and quote from this paper.
17. Ibid, p. 5.
18. University of Sunderland unpublished discussion paper, 'The University's Direct Contribution to the Local & Regional Economy'.
19. USER (University of Sunderland Environmental Report) (1996), p. 19.
20. This section is based on descriptive and promotional material produced by the University of Sunderland. I am grateful to the vice-chancellor, Dr Anne Wright, for permission to cite and quote from these publications.
21. Ibid.

8

The Impact of a New University on its Community: the University of Warwick

Michael Shattock

Unlike any other of the new greenfield universities created in the period between the end of the Second World War and the mid-1960s, the case for a new university in Coventry was championed by a mixed group of industrialists, trade unionists, civic authorities and a local intelligentsia of school teachers and college lecturers rather than by local and county notables. Keele might be regarded as an exception to this, but while the case brought forward for a university college in Stoke was certainly strongly supported by civic authorities, trade unionists and a local intelligentsia, the industrial commitment was weak, reflecting the economy of the area, and the political cohesion came from a shared vision of a leftward-leaning society rather than from the need to improve the skills base. In all the other cases to a greater or lesser extent (Sussex, East Anglia, Kent, Essex, Lancaster, York and Stirling) the activists were drawn from county families, civic dignitaries and church leaders. It was not surprising that Harold Wilson called them (and Warwick) the 'Baedeker universities' and compared them unfavourably with the upgraded colleges of advanced technology (Aston, Bath, Bradford City, Salford, and Surrey). Warwick's name put it into the Shakespearean category but its origins, in fact, lay firmly in Coventry, in support from the engineering companies associated with the motor car and aeronautics industries and from the local trade union movement, many of whose most senior members had taken over leadership roles in the city council (Shattock 1994).

Coventry had been told that it had to bring Warwickshire in to support the bid to have a chance of success in persuading the government of the strength of its case, and its political leaders had agreed to the name of Warwick as the price of achieving this. However, the passionate debates about what kind of university they wanted were conducted by chief executives and senior managers from Rootes, Hawker Siddeley, Courtaulds, Alfred Herbert, Jaguar and Coventry Gauge and Tool, trade unionists and city leaders whose backgrounds were in the Transport and General Workers'

Union (TGWU) and the engineering unions, and the principals and heads of the local teacher training college, technical colleges and grammar schools. When representatives of these groups eventually met the academic planning board appointed by the University Grants Council (UGC) to bring the university into existence, the gulf in attitude between the locals and the academics on the planning board was almost unbridgeable. The locals were explicit: what they wanted was a university which addressed the technological and labour problems of the Coventry sub-region, which would raise cultural levels, and which would complement and set the seal on the rebuilding and modernization of Coventry after the bombing of the city and the industries within it, who had played such a large part in the war effort. What the UGC group wanted, however, was a range of disciplines which complemented national provision (in which engineering, business education and biology, leading into medicine and agriculture, were already well-provided for) and a high quality undergraduate education which would be attractive to a national catchment. The reconciliation of these views was achieved only by the efforts of E.T. Williams (the chairman of the board and warden of Rhodes House in Oxford), Arnold Hall (managing director of Hawker Siddeley, a former professor from Imperial College, Fellow of the Royal Society and the founding vice-chancellor) and Jack Butterworth (an Oxford don whose attitude to relationships between universities and the real world made him an ideal appointment in such a situation). But the way these opposing views were bridged had a major impact on the university's subsequent development both in relation to its academic success and its contribution to the region (Shattock 1991).

It was only after considerable effort that the new university was able to persuade the UGC, which had previously rejected the proposal, to fund a development in engineering, and it was achieved only on the recommendation of a special UGC working party created to consult West Midlands industry on its needs. The university had to raise its own resources to initiate business education in defiance of the UGC, an action which ultimately provoked a change of heart at the UGC. Biological sciences was only funded two years after the university opened, when the Todd Commission recommended that Warwick might one day be a suitable site for a medical school. (Local support for a medical school remains strong and the university has now submitted a new bid for a medical school, 30 years after that initial decision.) But agriculture never gained support because the UGC was in the process of closing agricultural schools rather than creating new ones, even though the proximity of the headquarters of the Royal Agricultural Society of England, and of the National Vegetable Research Station (now HRI), and the strength of Warwickshire farming all made a strong local case.

In one important respect, however, the university's intention to realize the ambitions of its sponsors suffered a severe blow when in 1965 Crosland, then secretary of state, turned down an imaginative plan designed by Arnold Hall to merge the Lanchester College, then a regional technical college in the heart of Coventry which had particular strengths in engineering, with the university. This decision to maintain a separation between university and local education authority (LEA) led technical education, which was realized in the binary line, and the creation of 30 non-university polytechnics (of which the Lanchester College was one), dealt a body blow to Coventry's stated wish for 'a unitary and comprehensive system of higher education' which was 'the natural development of Coventry's desire for a technologically based system of higher education which had been their objective for the last five years and was supported by local industry' (Shattock 1991: 22).

The development of the university's regional impact was severely set back by this decision, not just because it vitiated a critical element of its overall plan, but because the disappointment of local political leaders caused them to turn to other solutions. The government's clear rejection of an imaginative proposal which had widespread local political and industrial support, the way it was done and the language of Crosland's Woolwich Speech (27 April 1965) ensured that the university retreated for a period into a more traditional and conventional view of its mission and the city and the county concentrated on rationalizing their existing commitments.

For the next 13 years the university concentrated on establishing departments, recruiting staff, attracting an increasingly well-qualified student intake, building up its academic profile and slowly developing the campus. It also acquired, in 1970, an unenviable reputation for student dissent fueled by Edward Thompson's attack on the alleged overdependence and subservience of the university to local industry (Thompson 1970). This had the effect of further distancing the university from its industrial heartland and from its origins. To most people involved in drawing up the bid for a university in Coventry, the institution that had emerged, ten years after it opened, was a severe disappointment. Located on an out of town greenfield site on land given by the city and the county, apparently cut off both from Coventry and from the centres of population in Warwickshire, it had little social impact. With only 4500 students, and its ambitious plans for growth repeatedly cut back by the exigencies of public expenditure, the university seemed a peripheral institution which had little connection with its local community. Indeed it could be and was argued that the university increasingly stood for fashionable middle class, left-wing values which were alien both to the much more down-to-earth pragmatism of the West Midlands and to the more radical forces which contributed so much to the trade union unrest which characterized the local industrial scene.

A number of factors combined to change this in the next five years, both within the university and within the local and regional community. It is not the purpose of this chapter to analyse in detail what they were. Some were the result of accidents of timing and the arrival on the scene of particular individuals and some came out of hard work to bring to fruition policies which seemed to have been overlaid by other interests for many years. But the overriding change was one of attitude brought about by the sharp economic decline in the West Midlands and the recognition in the university of its isolation at a time when its growing academic size and success gave it an opportunity to make an effective local and regional contribution. Indeed the decade from 1978 represented the period when the university began to realize for its community the hopes that many of those that had campaigned for a university had expressed. If we look back from the vantage point of a further decade we see a situation transformed where the university can be seen as the hub of a series of interlocking activities which have combined dramatically to change the economic, social and cultural landscape of its locality.

It is important to recognize that there have also been many forces outside the university which have contributed to this transformation, both in the national and global economies and in improvements to the local infrastructure such as the motorway system (the opening of the M40 had a dramatic impact on the local economy). But it was in this period that the university moved from being a peripheral to a major player in its community. It is not coincidental that the university has also doubled again in size in this last decade and has raised its position in the national university league tables to somewhere within the top ten British universities. The interrelationship of university success and local impact is difficult to assess but it is probably true that the location and size of a university are not in themselves simple guarantees of the quality of impact. Warwick's success, on the other hand, has certainly made it more of a magnet for a developmental role in the community.

The following sections try to identify the university's role under a series of headings. But the headings are to some extent artificial in that they suggest that the activities they encompass are very separate and do not have close interrelationships one with another. One important element of the university's success in its relationship with its local community is its ability to coordinate activities so that they mutually reinforce one another.

The Science Park

The West Midlands represents the heart of the British engineering industry. John Butcher MP, when he was a minister at the Department of Trade and Industry, sought to popularize the notion of the 'manufacturing corridor' extending from Telford across the country to Birmingham and Coventry and on to Rugby and Daventry. The Coventry, Warwickshire and Solihull areas in the 1970s were dominated by an automobile industry increasingly driven into recession by high wage costs, a failure to invest in new technology, international competition and its stubborn adherence to a 'low-tech', 'metal bashing' philosophy. By 1981 unemployment in Coventry had risen to 17.5 per cent and was still rising. The city council, encouraged by its chief executive, who had been much involved as planning officer in the early discussions about the physical planning of the university, opened a dialogue with the university to establish whether the university could offer any support or new ideas. The most tangible result was the proposal to create a science park with the explicit aim of attracting new industry and new technological skills into Coventry.

The Park was endowed with land leased to it partly by the university and partly by the city council. The university encouraged Warwickshire County Council to join the partnership and Coventry brought in the West Midlands County Council (which, after dissolution, transferred its shares to the West Midlands Enterprise Board) to create a company whose share capital was held in various proportions by the different partners. Unusually for a British science park Warwick was successful in attracting private capital in the form of a partnership with Barclays Bank to fund the first 'incubator' building intended to encourage the formation and growth of small high-tech companies. From a greenfield site of 14 acres adjoining the university in 1981, the park now encompasses 44 acres, houses 75 companies and provides direct employment for around 1500 people in a quality of environment which has proved to be a model for technology or business parks elsewhere in Coventry and Warwickshire. More important than the direct employment figures, however, is the fact that the Science Park made two other significant contributions. First, it attracted a range of small high-tech companies, mainly in the electronics field, who wanted to work with university departments and saw their profits coming from contracts from large low-tech parts of West Midlands industry. Their impact was transformational on the manufacturing processes of the region. Second, the well-publicized development of a focus for high-tech companies in Coventry represented a shot in the arm not just for the local economy but for the image of Coventry and its sub-region. Suddenly Coventry was no longer the backward-looking industrial city characterized by assembly lines, bad labour relations and poorly-constructed motor cars, but the base for a new diversified set of electronic, computer-based and even biotechnology companies. In reality of course the Science Park offered only a small revolution by comparison with the size of the local economy but it provided a new concept, a new growth point and in particular a new vision, which the local authorities and the university jointly and severally sought to represent on the national and international scene.

The Science Park has continued to make an important impact on the region. Restricted in its development on a single site and by the planning constraint which has prevented companies from moving downstream into manufacture on the Park itself, it has encouraged companies to move off the Park into nearby industrial or technology parks, further boosting the local economy. Two companies did just this: Parallax, a computer software company which joined the Park in 1992 with only eight staff, moved to a nearby business park in 1996 with its staff numbers increased to over a hundred, while Molins, one of the first occupants, moved off in the following year with a staff of around 120 to the Westwood Business Park next door.

Equally significant, the Science Park has begun establishing 'colonies' or outposts to serve as focuses for new industrial activity in locations away from the Park itself. Nearly 60 per cent of companies on the Science Park grew out of the first incubator building which has proved to be a uniquely effective forcing house for young technology-based companies. The first of the Science Park 'colonies' is an innovation centre based on the original incubator model, located on a technology park some eight miles away from the main park, adjoining the town of Warwick. The centre let all its space within six months of opening, and as a result an extension to the building is now being added. A second centre is being planned in a Coventry business park with the prospect of further projects to follow. Eventually it is intended to create a network of innovation centres linked to the main Park, each of which will offer a focus for new clusters of high-tech companies to form around. Since a condition of obtaining a tenancy on the Park has been strong links with a university department, this mushrooming growth of technology-based companies next door to the university has had an important secondary effect in keeping parts of the academic community engaged with the business problems of company formation and development. Several academics spend part of their working week in Science Park companies, and one – a senior professor of engineering and a former chairman of the department – has now left his academic post to become president of his company's new subsidiary in the USA.

Another development is the Science Park's interest in supporting small and medium sized enterprises (SMEs) in the region. It runs the largest Shell Technology and Enterprise Programme (STEP) scheme in the country, placing 60 or so science, engineering and computing undergraduates in small companies in the area for up to ten weeks in the summer vacation. It participates in the Linc Scheme through which 'business angels' provide venture capital to SMEs. This alone has brought the Science Park into contact with 150 SMEs in the region. It has piloted a scheme called TEAMSTART based on research carried out by Professor Storey, director of the SME Centre in the Warwick Business School, which brings venturers together into small groups which act as the nuclei for new technology-based SME formation. It has taken a leading role in RETEX, a scheme to diversify SMEs in the textile industry and in KONVER, which is designed to do the same for SMEs in the defence industry.

In one sense the limitation of the physical space on the Science Park has proved to be a blessing in disguise because it has forced the director and the board to look outwards for opportunities and new developments rather than simply working to fill a large piece of real estate. As a result the Science Park is greatly extending its regional significance and is leading a team drawn from Warwick and Birmingham Universities to design a regional innovation strategy. The Science Park sees itself playing a continuing role in the local economy and has set up a foundation based on the profits of the Science Park company to build up a new long-term source of funding for educational or research support for the region in years to come.

The Warwick Manufacturing Group (WMG)

Coincident with the establishment of the Science Park, the university appointed Kumar Bhattacharyya as professor of manufacturing systems, to establish a manufacturing group in the engineering department. The department had until then remained fairly small, partly because school leavers, put off by the image of British industry, were not applying for entry to engineering degrees in sufficient numbers to expand the department as planned, and partly because the department's academic expertise did not interface well with industry in the region. The university had for some time been actively trying to improve the position and the arrival of Bhattacharyya marked a dramatic change in direction. Nationally there was concern about the inadequate links between British science and engineering and British industry and the chairman of the Science and Engineering Research Council was convinced that Bhattacharyya's ideas deserved support. Although educated in India and with a Ph.D. in production engineering from Birmingham University, Bhattacharyya had also worked for Lucas Industries and was entirely at home in the West Midlands engineering environment.

His approach to working with industry was radically different from that of most academic engineers because he saw engineering problems more from the industrial and company than from the academic perspective and he took an holistic view of company development which incorporated ideas about the improvement of a company's technological base into an overall business strategy. He brought with him to Warwick the concept of the integrated graduate development programme, which Science and Engineering Research Council (SERC) was prepared initially to fund, and which aimed to train well-qualified young science graduates already in industry for a masters degree in manufacturing through concentrated one-week residential courses interspersed through their first two or three years in their company. The essence of the scheme was the establishment of a consortium of companies willing to share technological know-how and to contribute to the teaching of such a programme. The close relationships which this programme and its many successors demanded with industry at all levels, sustained by large industrially-supported research programmes which were not afraid to tackle development as well as research problems revolutionized the relationships between the department and industry. When the managing director of Rover cars said publicly that his company, then in the early stages of turnaround to profitability, took no fundamental decisions about business strategy without consulting Professor Bhattacharyya and his SERC-supported teaching company group he was flagging up a depth of relationship between industry and the academic community that had previously been unknown, at least in the West Midlands where arm's-length relationships and some mutual suspicion had previously been the norm.

The creation of the WMG had an important impact on the success of the Science Park because around a third of the first companies to seek tenancies were linked or were anxious to link themselves with WMG. Many of these were from overseas, both from the USA and from continental Europe. Thus, Computervision, a company which first developed out of Massachusetts Institute of Technology (MIT), came to form a fundamental relationship with WMG and with Rover from its Science Park base. When in January 1995 Computervision announced the formation of its $40 million collaboration with WMG it was reflecting the extension of the extraordinary relationship it had formed with the group and initially with West Midlands industry into continental Europe and the Pacific Rim. The strength of these industrial relationships led Rover and Rolls Royce to build an advanced technology centre next to the engineering building on the university campus to expand research collaboration with WMG, and to an expansion of Computervision on the Science Park. With the decision to extend the high-level post-experience training from the major manufacturers down to their suppliers, the WMG found itself in regular contact with over 300 companies and an enormous additional range of SMEs. With a rapid build-up to around 300 masters and D.Eng. students a year, almost every major manufacturing company in the West Midlands now has a core group of senior staff who have been trained at Warwick and who maintain relationships with WMG through research collaboration, training consortia or industrial 'clubs'. These relationships have had a fundamental impact on the modernization of the engineering industry of the West Midlands, not just because of the technological innovation, the re-engineering of company structures, and the creation of supply chain relationships, but because the shared culture of links with WMG has created new attitudes to the technological/business interface and to the globalization of manufacturing.

Post-experience training

One of the by-products of WMG's plans to develop residential programmes was the conversion of a hall of residence, Arden House, into an executive training centre. Experience in managing this venture led to further investments by the university into purpose-built centres (Radcliffe and Scarman Houses), which between them provide 350 hotel-style bedrooms, catering and teaching facilities, open on an all the year round basis for internal university use or external lettings. With companies' recognition of the need to increase their commitment to training and staff development these centres have played a significant role in building university-industry relationships. Several companies have contributed capital to retain dedicated suites within the centres for their own training purposes, while many academic departments have followed WMG into the field of post-experience training. The most notable of these is the Warwick Business School, revitalized by the appointment of Professor George Bain to its chairmanship in the mid-1980s. Not only does the Business School run a large short-course programme but also a major part-time MBA programme (in addition to its full-time and distance learning MBAs) which link it closely to local and regional industry and many public sector bodies. In addition its SME Centre has become a major regional resource, not only for the training of entrepreneurs but as a research centre, one of whose functions is the analysis of data on the progress of SMEs in the West Midlands. The SME Centre cooperates closely with the Science Park both in advising start-up companies and offering training to their staff and also in relation to the Science Park's international activities, particularly in its European Union (EU) funded training programme for science parks in Russia (see below).

University collaboration with industry is not new. Because Warwick is a research-intensive university and because it is strong across the sciences, its research capability is important to the region, but apart from WMG there is probably nothing particularly distinctive about it apart from the special relationships with some companies on the Science Park. It is always assumed in the literature that technology transfer takes place through research, but Warwick's experience is that the most effective form of technology transfer occurs through post-experience training either through short courses or through part-time masters programmes. About 40 per cent of Warwick's total student population are postgraduates and about 70 per cent of these are studying in vocational fields. If one adds the vocational short-course numbers to part-time masters students, around 6600 employed people are taking vocational programmes at the university each year. This represents a considerable resource for a regional economy which has, over the last decade, recovered the competitiveness of the post-war boom years.

Education

One turning point in the university's relationship with its community was the take-over of the Coventry College of Education in 1978. The principal of the college, Joan Browne, had played a major role in the discussions which led up to the creation of the university but the college, like the Lanchester College, had remained part of the Coventry LEA. However, the run-down of colleges of education in the 1970s led to discussions as to whether the Coventry College should merge either with the Lanchester Polytechnic or with the university. When the dust had settled on the university merger, the university discovered it had inherited an entirely new set of relationships with local schools, with teacher unions, and with chief education officers in respect to in-service (or post-experience) courses for teachers in Coventry, Warwickshire and Solihull. From looking at education and schools entirely from the point of view of its national catchment of student applicants the university suddenly found itself involved in all the problems of schools in deprived urban areas and in the debates about the training and retraining of the teaching workforce.

Inevitably this led to a growing involvement of the university with schools' policies. Every year 60 or 70 Warwick graduates take teaching posts in the area and maintain contact thereafter with the Institute of Education in the university. When Warwick students go into schools on teaching placement there is a strong chance that one or more of the staff will have trained at Warwick. The university's education library remains a focal point for teachers in the area and encourages school-based research in collaboration with the Institute, while the Institute's in-service training activities constitute an important exercise in partnership with LEAs. The Institute works closely with the National Council for Educational Technology (NCET), the body primarily concerned with implementing information technology (IT) into school curricula, which is located just across the road on the Science Park. The NCET collaborates with the Institute in research and in the development of IT for teachers. This offers obvious benefits for local schools and illustrates again the way that the interrelationship of activities created or generated by the university can enrich its local environment.

The university's involvement in education in the region does not end here, however. In 1981 in the wake of the merger with the Coventry College, the university took over responsibility for adult and continuing education for Coventry, Warwickshire and Solihull from the University of Birmingham. This has grown into a major activity, with 7000 people taking open studies programmes in centres on or off the campus including a special centre in Hillfields where the greatest concentration of ethnic minorities are to be found in Coventry. The West Midlands remains an area of considerable social and educational disadvantage with a low participation rate in higher education (HE) and, in addition to its open studies programmes, the university has launched part-time and 2+2 undergraduate degree programmes to provide routes into the university outside the traditional A levels.

The most ambitious and innovative of these schemes is the 2+2 degree which is taught through a partnership with the nine further education (FE) colleges in the Coventry, Warwickshire and Solihull areas and with Evesham College. These colleges are members of the Warwick Community University Board and their staff are encouraged to take part in university staff development programmes and to collaborate in the joint university/FE college research consortium. The degrees involve close liaison between the university and the colleges, with the university library and other facilities, including the government's access funds being available to students in their first two college-based years. The students, mostly women between the ages of 25 and 35 from educationally disadvantaged backgrounds, perform outstandingly well academically in comparison with the traditional university intake, once their financial problems can be overcome. On graduation these students move on into professional careers in the local community or into higher degree work, outcomes which would have been inconceivable before they had applied to enter the university. Although the numbers are relatively small the well-publicized evidence of their success offers a powerful message back to the community from which they have come.

The arts

Before the university's Arts Centre opened the only significant live performing arts location in the area, apart from the Royal Shakespeare Company (RSC) at Stratford, was the Belgrade Theatre in Coventry. The Warwick Arts Centre now represents the major arts venue in the Midlands offering a concert hall, two theatres, an art gallery and a film theatre. It attracts over 250,000 paying visitors a year and has a box office turnover of over £1 million. Its audience is drawn from as far north as Stoke and as far south as Oxford, but is primarily from a 20-mile radius of the university. The university orchestras and choirs, which are also open to non-members of the university, also involve significant numbers from the community. The Arts Centre acts as a major shop-window for the university and as a bridge to the community. With an audience of up to 1400 for a subscription concert, together with a theatre audience of 450 and a film audience of 300, the Arts Centre can attract over 2000 people to the campus in the evenings. The audience browses in the university bookshop, eats in the Arts Centre restaurant, and visits the Mead gallery in the Arts Centre. On a campus which has about 14,000 students, 5000 of whom are resident on campus, an external audience of this size adds to the sense of busyness and bustle after teaching ends. The university is no longer the isolated, out of town location of the 1970s, but the social, educational and cultural hub of the Coventry, Warwickshire and Solihull communities in a way that would have amazed and gratified its original advocates. Probably nothing has sold Coventry more effectively to the employees of companies moving to the Westwood Business Park which adjoins the university than the presence of the Arts Centre, with its promise of high-grade cultural entertainment delivered with metropolitan style and pizzazz. In a very genuine sense the Arts Centre is regarded possessively by the community whether for its music, theatre and film performances or for its school programmes, Saturday morning drama classes or craft displays. It is probably the most potent symbol of the university's accessibility to the wider public.

The university as a bridgehead to the global community

The visitor to the West Midlands at any time up to the late 1970s would have noted that outside Birmingham, and setting aside the tourists in Stratford, the region did not connect well with the wider international community. The success of Birmingham Airport and of the National Exhibition Centre have played a significant role in changing this, but the university's success has also played its part. One obvious component is the 1800 overseas students who attend the university, but another is the role of WMG in taking its masters programmes overseas for delivery in Hong Kong, India, Thailand,

Malaysia and South Africa. As manufacturing becomes a global business the WMG has responded to the call of overseas markets. But these are two-way flows. When the university Business School's 1800 distance learning MBA students fly in for their compulsory one week formal in-house programme on the campus, they bring not just local spending power but a link with the international business community. When delegations from Indian, Malaysian or Chinese industry visit the university they are also keen to do business with the university's industrial partners. A joint Science Park/Business School team are not just training Russian science park entrepreneurs and managers, they are also tapping into Russian scientific expertise. Jointly funded programmes with science parks on the continent bring new companies to the West Midlands and the Science Park itself has attracted Computervision, Morton International, Breed Technologies, Buelher Krautkramer, Advanced Bionics Corporation, Concentra, Leeman Labs, Schmitt Industries and Sun Microsystems from the USA, as well as companies from France and Germany. When the prime minister, Tony Blair, spoke by videoconferencing link from the Warwick campus to WMG's partners in Malaysia and Hong Kong he was representing the region's profile as well. When the prime minister of Malaysia visited the university he also met groups of senior West Midlands industrialists. When the Moscow State Orchestra or the Berlin Philharmonic play in the Arts Centre they are emphasizing that the university is opening its community to a wider world. Whether it is through its academic links, the cosmopolitan nature of its staff or the impact of its wider activities, the university represents the most important point of connection with the global economy in this part of the West Midlands.

Conclusion

So what can we say about the university's economic, social and cultural impact on its community? Perhaps the first thing to note is that the gift of 250 acres each from Coventry and Warwickshire for the site of the university probably represented the best economic investment either local authority ever made. In under 35 years the university has grown to employ 3600 people, making it the fifth largest employer in the area. Its success and particularly the Science Park's success, has led to an expansion of Coventry towards the west side of the city, with a new city business park adjoining the Science Park which has attracted the kind of professional organizations which, without the university as a magnet, would never have left London or the South-East. The very size of the university now makes it an important player in the local scene. The bus services it sponsors to bring its students onto the campus from Leamington, Kenilworth and Coventry (the previous public services having virtually collapsed) provide the most regular and reliable public transportation system in the area. Its 2500 university-leased flat places in the community act as a guarantee of low rents in the housing market. As a local resident your children can be taught to swim in the university pool or do gymnastics in the Gymnastics Centre, can be taught by a Warwick graduate in their school, and can be brought to the Arts Centre or to special schools' events organized by the Arts Centre's education officer. You can yourself take continuing education classes or as a company employee attend executive training courses or masters programmes in the Business School, the engineering or other departments, or you can simply go to the Arts Centre for concerts, theatre, film and its gallery. Warwick is not a community university in the sense that it is orientated primarily towards the community but a major international university which has tried to put back into the community what the community itself looked for when it bid for a university. In doing so it has broken free from the constraints initially imposed on it by national policy, and by working with local and regional partners in all kinds of ways it has enriched both itself and the community. When the commercial league tables point to Leamington Spa as one of the most prosperous towns in Britain they point to the university effect. And when the university does well it can recognize that part of its success reflects the qualities of the community it has itself helped to create which has provided long-term support for its staff and students. If there is a message in this it is that universities which engage wholeheartedly with their communities may initially be doing it out of a very proper idealism, but if they do it well, they will obtain a substantial return.

Warwick's success in engaging with and responding to its local and regional community is not accidental. It recognized in the late 1970s that events had combined to isolate it from its community and that in the modern era a successful university should be able to demonstrate that its success was based on something more than a narrow base of research excellence and the ability to attract the best students: it had to show itself to be useful as well as being excellent and it had to have friends as well as admirers. The university consciously adopted a policy of relating better to its community and sought to coordinate its various activities so that success in one area fed into another. It did not adopt a formal strategic plan to put this into effect, but it corporately encouraged partnership, collaboration and a sense of involvement. What it quickly identified was an eagerness in the community to respond. Partly this reflected a reawakening of the disappointed hopes for the new university in the 1960s, and partly simply the recognition that a university willing to play a part in its community could bring something different and could open windows to a wider world.

It is perfectly possible to prepare an economic assessment of Warwick's impact on its local and regional economy: the economic tools and the data are readily to hand. But the purpose of this chapter has been to assess a wider impact that takes into account the social, the educational and the cultural, as well as the industrial and directly economic. In the age of mass higher education, world universities are going to be judged by society on much broader criteria than the traditional academic norms. Warwick can lay some claim to be able to meet such a wider agenda.

References

Shattock, M. (1991) *Making a University*. Warwick, University of Warwick.
Shattock, M. (1994) *The UGC and the Management of British Universities* pp. 73–80. Buckingham, Open University Press.
Thompson, E.P. (1970) (ed.) *Warwick University Ltd*. Harmondsworth, Penguin.

9

Salford University: an Historical Industrial Partnership

Peter Brandon

The context

Established as a university from a College of Advanced Technology in 1969, and set at the very centre of the historic source of the worldwide industrial revolution in Manchester, Salford was bound to find an affinity with Britain's manufacturing base. At least that is the theory and there is more than a grain of truth in this statement. However it requires more than a geographical location, or even an academic tradition, to realize a change in a university to the point where it becomes a role model for a large sector of UK universities. Indeed Salford's vision and application has had an impact beyond its natural allies to more traditional education centres and has influenced government thinking, affecting much of its education and research policy. Words and phrases like 'capability', 'relevance' and 'coincidence of purpose with industry' are familiar to those engaged in the Salford revolution which occurred in the 1980s. Reviewing the change of the vocabulary, the re-prioritization of university objectives and the general engagement of industry from the late 1990s perspective, it is difficult to imagine the culture of the early 1980s when these matters were barely discussed.

We now have in the UK a pluralistic university system which is only just learning to come to terms with its own diversity. The conversion of polytechnics to universities, the greater selectivity in research funding and the movement towards a 'level playing field' for teaching funds are creating an uncertainty about the role of universities which is probably more an internal problem to the universities themselves than it is to the public perception. Many universities wish to rigorously oppose the change from the status quo, while others still aspire to the 'ivy league' model without challenging its contribution to the wider community. What is clear is that for many universities the way forward is not to emulate a past glory, but to sensitize their vision to the wider market which now beckons. The high unemployment of the 1980s and the massive growth in the participation rate in higher education (HE) have created new demands from the student body. In addition, the industrial base is requiring new knowledge and skills related to the new workplace, and government is demanding more accountability. In particular this means more accountability as to how the university serves the economic interests of the nation. The government White Paper *Realising our Potential* (HMSO 1993) clearly points to a vision for universities which encourages closer links with industry and the community to enable 'wealth creation' and improved 'quality of life'. Under the Conservative government the emphasis was most definitely on the former, whereas the Labour government appears, at least at present, to treat them both equally.

Levers for change

The contribution universities make to the local economy was not articulated in the late 1970s and early 1980s, mainly because it appeared unnecessary. Why focus on issues which had not appeared on the agenda of governments since the war? Interest in this aspect had to wait until much later and a study conducted in 1994 (Deas *et al.* 1995) suggested that the four Manchester universities, including Salford, generated £468 million within Greater Manchester and are a major factor in jobs and job creation. However the same report addressed the views of academics and industrialists and notes the following:

> The perceptions of many of those outside the university sphere, however, raise questions about how widely the collaborative role of the universities [within the region] has yet been appreciated and of the degree to which the economic and cultural roles of the four universities within the locality and region have impinged on the views of those external to the university sector. Doubts were expressed about whether the universities spread themselves too thinly or were involved in more than a token fashion. Scepticism was voiced about whether universities could 'deliver' what was promised and there was criticism of the opacity and complexity of university structures. Countering this, many of those from within the Universities felt that business and industry had expectations of universities that were unrealistic: universities are businesses, faced with the same need to make profits as was the private sector; they are not primarily in the business of vocational training; their research skills and advice should not be seen as free goods; the complexity of their structures is no greater than that of any big business; there is an onus on business and industry to learn more about the ways in which universities operate and about their policy and their financial imperatives.
>
> (Deas *et al.* 1995: 5)

The above paragraph illustrates the debate which still continues, and the differing perspectives suggest that the cultures of universities and businesses continue to be seen in some quarters as being distinct from one another.

Bridging the gap remains a challenge for all those who are concerned with the economic well-being of the nation. Even now, Salford's 1980s revolution seems strange to many. None of these great issues affecting mission were evident to the universities of the late 1970s and early 1980s. Neither was the change in student per capita funding, which had resulted in a reduction of 26 per cent over the four years prior to 1996. Most universities in the 1980s were continuing to pursue learning as a goal in its own right without significant reference to the needs of industry. Only in the polytechnic sector were there signs that addressing the vocational needs of the nation was a high priority. It is against this background that the particular ethos of Salford began to evolve. Here was a university with a technological background, strong in engineering and science and undertaking largely applied research. It seemed to be doing all the things that successive governments required during the 1970s, including addressing Harold Wilson's 'white heat of the technological revolution'.

When the shock hit the university in 1981, it was in a period of transition from one vice-chancellor to another, and the university was quietly developing its applied research strengths with a number of industrial partners. The shock was that there were imposed the largest financial cuts to be placed on any one university this century: 43 per cent over a period of three years and no discussion! There is no doubt that a cut of 43 per cent focuses the mind and gets the adrenalin moving. Professor John Ashworth, the vice-chancellor designate, was aware of the oncoming calamity, at least in outline, through his work in the Cabinet Office which he was about to leave. It did not deter him from the challenge which (he said) was to develop a university which was viable and, equally importantly, relevant to the society it sought to serve. The Cabinet Office experience had given more than just early warning of the impending cuts. It had also given valuable insight into the thinking of the new Conservative government and its leader, Margaret Thatcher. The new regime viewed public expenditure on universities as an investment which should have clear pay-offs in the medium-term. The pay-offs could be of many kinds, but primarily an economic return to 'UK Limited' was required. The level of discussion among the universities of this time on this issue was woefully low and a new model for a university was long overdue. John Ashworth and his colleagues at Salford determined that they would address the cuts, but at the same time they would mark out the way forward for at least some universities of the future. They realized that there were many in the educational establishment who would be against them. The old values were revered and as we have noted earlier are still continuing today. There was no intention to create a panacea or template for all HE institutions. Indeed the reverse was true. Salford would carve out its own market niche (a term not prevalent in universities in those days) and would use this new identity to benefit business, industry and the community as well as ensure its own survival.

For Ashworth, the Victorian institutionalization and reform of our universities had led to a sharp distinction between what is described as 'education' and what is described as 'training' – a distinction that was not perceived as helpful to many people in the UK. 'Education' was presented as being at a higher level and reflecting the best liberal tradition. 'Training' was something those with a less formal and respectable education undertook and was largely to be gained by in-service learning. These two traditions divided the country both economically and socially. The discussion revealed itself in many ways and often separated those who were based in the scholarly traditions of the library and those whose source material was the workshop and the design studio. As Ashworth put it, 'The pinnacle of success for a University student (in 1985) is to be invited to stay, as a scholar, inside the University's walls – success for a student in the other tradition is not to stay, but to go out into the world to change and, we all hope, improve it' (Ashworth 1985: 236). These traditions, it could be argued, went further and affected the British financial and corporate system. Hutton (1996) described this as 'gentlemanly capitalism', which places particularly high social status on the less risky, invisible sources of income generated in trading and financial activity, rather than on production. These divisions are not found in the other successfully developed, or indeed developing countries, and could have been one of the underlying issues resulting in the perceived British economic malaise during the late 1970s and early 1980s. The question for Salford was whether it was possible to reconcile these two established traditions.

To tackle these issues in a university setting, Ashworth, together with Stuart Bosworth, the Salford University registrar, and their pro-vice-chancellors, decided to rethink the university role in the context of the needs of the business community. They wanted to educate for 'capability' and in doing so they wanted to engage the industrial and business communities. Within 'capability' they included the exercise of creative skills, the competence to undertake and complete tasks and the ability to cope with everyday life in cooperation with others, both now and in the future. This is no easy task as it affects the changing of long-held views, the creation of new allegiances and significant organizational and managerial implications for any university wanting to go down this route. There is no set path but varying approaches and mechanisms can be used depending on circumstances. For some universities it will be better not to make the attempt if their members do not have the collective will to turn a policy of fundamental change into practice.

For some it will be easier, and those universities who were previously polytechnics or Colleges of Advanced Technology will have a stronger ethos towards vocational training. They may also have a more executive centralized style of management enabling them to take matters forward more quickly. What they may lack, however, is the strong research ethos which can engage the industrial and business community at the level of creative ideas and innovation and build partnerships from this base. The four-year research assessment exercise, where funds often follow traditional academic performance, has not helped in establishing this new style partnership with commerce and industry as developed by Salford.

There is one further point that needs to be made. There had been calls for several years requesting more 'relevance' in the curriculum. While the Salford team recognized this as an important component they believed that the problem was more fundamental. It was not just tailoring the teaching content to the needs of industry, but a full and proper 'engagement' with the business community that was required. This would be a two way flow of inputs and outputs at all levels of university activity which would ensure continuous feedback and participation for years to come. The boundary between the university and where practice of its knowledge took place was to become blurred to the point where there was a natural progression of knowledge from each sector into the other without bureaucratic or other constraints. It was this willingness to break through the traditional barriers which was welcomed by the business community and resulted in the support which the initiative was to gain. Wherever obstacles might occur every attempt was made to reduce or remove the problem to ensure a harmonious relationship.

The new approach

The Salford management team in 1981 had some stark decisions to make on the announcement of the cuts. While they had to undertake a root and branch review of all their activities and many staff were given favourable terms to take voluntary early retirement, they had to act to take the university forward. The alternative was to manage decline, and even the possible closure of Salford. The response was typical of the university, even today. It would cut through the traditional barriers to industry and business collaboration, think afresh about what it could do to enable a strong working relationship to develop and carve out its own particular ethos based on a strong commitment to engagement with the community it served.

To take this forward it was vital that the rest of the university was behind the initiative. The management realized that you cannot manage a relationship with industry in isolation from the rest of its activities. It is absolutely vital that the staff of the university know what it is they are trying to achieve and understand what is expected of them. A full and frank debate was introduced soon after the cuts were announced, and by November 1982 the senate had formally approved a statement of aims and objectives for the university which summarized and codified its conclusions under the three headings of teaching, research and 'technology and skill transfer'. Their statements made clear that 'the University seeks in particular to serve, through teaching and research, the best interests of a) industry, commerce and the public service and b) of each of its students' (University of Salford, Senate Minutes, November 1992). Each department had then, in turn, to adopt (formally) specific statements of its own aims and objectives in a form that was useful in managerial terms. There had to be a 'dynamic' in the statements in order that difficult decisions could be made about reprioritization, reallocation of resources and the role of staff. The latter was significant because each member of staff had a role and task to play within the overall system and the management had a responsibility to support, assess and reward those individuals appropriately. An important part of the mechanisms devised for collaboration were the incentives, often in the form of consultancy, which would reward and retain key members of staff.

Not every member of staff could undertake the full portfolio of collaboration and it was recognized, by implication, that there needed to be parity of esteem between the three headings of teaching, research, and technology and skill transfer mentioned above. However, rewards should be there for demonstrable achievement in activities connected with the university's relations with industry as much as with conventional university activities. This in turn required recognition through the promotion procedures, career development schemes and the resource allocation models to ensure that the system supported the vision.

In conjunction with the internal changes it was important that the business and other communities were convinced that the university had the commitment to deliver its vision. A conventional public relations exercise was launched by the vice-chancellor to explain the increased drive for collaboration and to promote to a much wider audience, including the government, that here was a university that believed what it said and was taking active measures to ensure that it met the needs of the extended community. This message, coupled with the pithy nature of the vice-chancellor's delivery, had a major impact for the whole of the early and middle 1980s. John Ashworth was in regular demand for comment, ministers frequently visited the university and business looked at the university as one of their own. Of course this could be only a second order aspect of the strategy, however important it was to winning the battle. The primary imperative was to build the systems and structures which give reality to true collaborations. If this reality was to be achieved it was important to have at the heart of the university a high status, high profile organization with which industry could identify and which was a visible sign of the university's commitment.

The purpose of such an organization was, and still is, to develop and foster continuing relationships with outside bodies. These relationships would be varied with differing demands from different organizations and in every case would require nurturing to ensure the collaboration had useful purpose and was sustainable. The body that performs this function is CAMPUS (Campaign for the University of Salford), organized as a charitable trust with a board of trustees, a director and a small group of staff. This enabled the organization to initiate projects but was of insufficient size to undertake them itself – avoiding the problem of a competitor organization with an independent mission from the university. Once initiated and brought to maturity a project needed to be released and operated by the university's established structures. It was not, and is not, primarily a fund-raising organization. If CAMPUS initiatives create customer-centred type contracts then they can be handed over to, and managed by, the university company (now Salford University Business Services Ltd).

There is little doubt that the initiative to create CAMPUS has been significant in building relationships with a wide spectrum of organizations nationally and within the North-West. For any university wishing to build the bridge between industry and academia it is likely that they will need to create a similar dedicated group whose primary function is to ensure that the interests of the university's industrial friends are represented on policy-making bodies in the university. One aspect of policy includes research. Unless a university is very rich it will have to make choices, and prioritize between competing research activities. It is not always easy for a committee composed exclusively of academics to make the hard decisions which are often necessary on research priorities. In the early 1980s CAMPUS and our industrial friends were able to give Salford help on these issues. In time this help became less formal as the ethos of the university began to change in line with the new mission. In the early days a CAMPUS Academic Venture and Enterprise (CAVE) fund was formed from different sources of income and was used to support research activities of members of staff. In the first three years the CAVE fund had allocated nearly £1 million to some 75 projects selected from three times that number submitted by members of staff.

The CAMPUS office used the university's industrial friends to make recommendations. The final decision was taken by a committee of academics and industrialists thus involving the industrialists to help in the research policy of the University of Salford. Ashworth (1985) noted that this innovation did not lead to applied research being funded preferentially but on occasion did lead to novel activities some of which were overtly commercial or market orientated. In addition the CAVE committee functioned as a technology transfer mechanism which allowed a natural and smooth transmission of knowledge into the market-place. It should be pointed out that there was a substantial sum of other research money also provided which was distributed to departments to maintain their research infrastructure and to follow their own priorities.

Other initiatives

Other initiatives were also taken at this time. A novel kind of professorial appointment known as 'the integrated chair' was established by senate in 1982. Holders of such posts had and have managerial responsibility both in the university (where they are based in an academic department and are full members of senate) and in the university's industrial or commercial partner. The salary and other costs of the chair are shared between the university and the industrial firm in the same ratio as the individual professor divides his or her time. Firms such as British Gas, British Aerospace, Unilever and Dainichi-Sykes Robotics were some of the first to engage in this way. One of the most interesting features of these appointments was the way in which the holders were prepared to assist in the development of curriculum which was not expected at the time of inauguration. Another initiative was the use of any surplus funds in the CAMPUS office to fund temporary promotions for members of staff who excelled in areas allied to CAMPUS activities or who met criteria set by the CAMPUS trustees. In addition a CAMPUS reward scheme was set up whereby those members of staff who take on work on behalf of CAMPUS can be rewarded by having access to funds for professional purposes, for example, conference fees, travel, equipment or books. Each member firm has an academic contact within the university whose responsibility it is to liaise with staff and provide the gateway into the university's knowledge and activities.

Other examples of the changing ethos can be found in new initiatives which 'spin' out from the new mission. In July 1984 the Butcher Committee's report on graduate information technology (IT) skill shortages was launched and called for new sorts of partnership between HE and industry. By September of that year in conjunction with its industrial friends the university had submitted a successful fully costed proposal to government for a new IT institute. The proposed institute was financed in part by direct government contract for an initial five-year period and became a self-standing unit within the university, analogous in some respects to a medical school. It had a director who was also a professor of the university and a core cadre of full-time tenured university teachers, but a substantial part of the staffing effort came initially from the National Computing Centre and from collaborating industrial firms. Its mission was to produce a new kind of graduate trained in IT-based skills and its management structure would be overtly and explicitly teaching and mission orientated. In time this mission has been adapted very successfully to include applied research for various sections of the UK economy.

A further example was the construction management course in the Department of Surveying. This course was and is supported by the ten leading construction companies in the UK who provide some management and teaching of the course curriculum, sponsorship of students and a contribution to the course costs. In return for their contribution they have a major say in the course content, the choice of students and the quality levels expected. It is a 'closed' course limited to the contractors and represents a real partnership between the university and the firms. One interesting innovation in the curriculum was to include an outward bound course at John Ridgeways Adventure School to test the leadership characteristics of the students. For survivors it is the reference point for all their future activities!

The illustrations above are examples of a change in culture which has resulted in a marked change in attitude within the institution. The pioneering work of John Ashworth and his team in bridging the gap between industry and the university has continued to this day. The fact that it was successful has helped to change the ethos within Salford. Externally it is still perceived as one of the universities closest to Britain's industrial community. Many others have followed, government policy has reinforced the trend, and there is every indication that it will continue. That is not to say that things have stood still for the last decade – far from it – but the foundation of a rather special ethos is still there.

The university company

It would not be right to cover the historical development of Salford's relationship with business without mentioning the role of the university company known at the time as Salford University Industrial Centre Ltd (SUIC) and now Salford University Business Services Ltd. This company had been in existence for most of the 1970s with a respectable turnover, for that time, of around half a million pounds a year. It was clear that in the new mission it would undertake the commercial and consultancy role within the new links which were inappropriate for the university to undertake. It also had a role to play in retaining key innovative and knowledgeable staff who might be tempted elsewhere – particularly at the time of the cuts. Consultancy was seen as being part of technology transfer in the new mission and was an integral part of the links with the business community. It enabled academics to enhance their salary. This was not something to be shied away from but something to be emphasized. Any new member of staff coming to the university from another would have been surprised at the freedom and encouragement given to consultancy under the new regime. In addition to the development, marketing and management of applied academic research and innovation, the company acted as an access point in the North-West for consultancy and management of schemes initiated by the Department of Trade and Industry (DTI). This new work also engaged other academics from other institutions and there was no preferential prioritization for Salford staff. The focus was on business planning and problem solving, the themes for the DTI in those days, and the turnover grew rapidly. By the end of the 1980s it had reached around £10 million per annum, had involved the development of a business park with English Estates (with tenants selected to suit the innovative culture) and eventually the establishment of a venture capital company with Salford City Council. It also engaged in other venture funds with Manchester Airport. This rapid growth was of major benefit to the university with covenanted profits adding to the university research fund, but it also reinforced the image of Salford as a university which was aware of business. The staff benefited by gaining extra income, expertise in management of the development, marketing and business acumen and of course had the extra cover provided by the company's professional indemnity insurance. In the recent recession of the early 1990s, during which time there was also a change of DTI policy, the company has had to rethink its strategy but is still an active partner to the university's business links and plays a very important role in CAMPUS and many new university initiatives.

Change in the 1990s

If the 1980s was a period of change for Salford and some other universities then the 1990s brought major change to the whole sector. 'Efficiency gains' were demanded by the government, quality assurance was demanded by the funding councils and accountability was required for the investment of public money in a manner not seen before. The participation rate in HE rose to one in three school-leavers from one in seven previously, and the knock-on effect was reduced funding per student and a requirement that students contribute to their maintenance (and now their tuition fees as well). League tables abstracted from the statistical data prepared by universities were circulated widely despite the dubious nature of some of the criteria selected. Funding began to follow the student, thus creating a market which was nevertheless heavily regulated. Industrialists were called in to provide direction to research councils, to guide government department funding and to aid general prioritization through mechanisms such as Technology Foresight. The Dearing Report from the National Committee of Inquiry into Higher Education (NCIHE 1997) was published, and its impact will be felt for some time to come. It is too early to judge outcome, but there is a clear thrust for lifelong learning linking with business and the community which encourages the Salford approach outlined previously.

All these changes have and will affect university mission and its relationship to business and the community to a greater or lesser extent. The reduction in funding, for example, has meant larger class sizes, more marking of student work per member of staff and, therefore, less time for staff to engage in links with the business community. The reduction in equipment funding has meant that the equipment infrastructure with which to provide the facilities to liaise and link with industry has been severely undermined. Increased accountability, too, has meant less time for staff to undertake the bridging role. Nevertheless, despite the problems, universities in general have realized the need to work with industry and the community and have invested accordingly, albeit on a more selective basis. The changes have not always been obvious to our colleagues from business or indeed the government, some of whom may still be carrying in their heads an image of the universities they went to some 30 years previously.

Perhaps the most dramatic change in the early 1990s was the explicit linking of research performance of universities to the amount of income they received from the higher education funding councils (HEFCs). The research assessment exercise of 1992 was the third in all, but the first to assess every subject area within every university that chose to submit and provide a grading which determined the funds to be received by each university. This was continued in 1996 but only with those above a Grade 2 gaining funds. The government argument was simple: there is a limited sum of money available; we should reward excellence; and we should concentrate funds where success has been proven. While this exercise had many strong points, and on balance has achieved much, it also had some downsides. What is considered to be excellent and a proven success depends on from what perspective the judgement is to be made. In the 1996 exercise chairmen and their panels were specifically instructed not to assess 'the relevance' of the submitted work. This was a research quality exercise and not a measure of how it benefited industry or the community. With the exception of one or two of the assessment panels (e g the Built Environment which set up an industry sub-panel) the input from commerce or community was small. Consequently the academic filter could well have skewed the assessment towards a certain type of research and penalized some of the applied research of greatest benefit to industry.

The 1996 exercise was the fourth and Salford's managed approach to research, described later, did have a positive impact. However, the policy adopted by the university in the 1980s of working in collaboration with industry did create a major problem in the previous three exercises when viewed through a traditional academic filter. Salford believes these collaborative links, which had resulted in so much good applied research throughout the 1980s and before, were undervalued by those who took a traditional standpoint. This may still be a problem and certainly there are many new universities (previously polytechnics) who would take this view. The result may be that the applied research, particularly in embryonic disciplines and embryonic research groups will be decimated by the lower grades and lower funding obtained. If Salford University had known the criteria to be employed and the linking of funding that followed, it is debatable whether it would have developed its collaborative strategy in quite the same way during the 1980s. It set out to be different and relevant and when funds were not linked to research gradings it could afford to be so. The previous funding regime had provided the flexibility to be innovative.

Managing for sustainable collaboration

The new problem for Salford in the 1990s was how to adapt its existing structures and collaborative alliances to suit the new external environment and address the requirements of the research assessment panels. In addition, the university realized that it had to manage its research effort as a major function of university activity. Previously, departments were the focal point for research. If research was to be given a significant place in university priorities then it needed to permeate all management decision making from the senior management team to the individual researcher. To gain this level of recognition it had to be seen to be important and needed to be an agenda item in all academic policy decision making. Further, the well-established links with industry and the community which were largely focused on the research activity needed to be reinforced.

Fortunately the network with industry already created could be used to assist in the restructuring necessary. A new pro-vice-chancellor role for research and postgraduate activity was created, and working with the new vice-chancellor, Tom Husband, together with their senior colleagues, the two consulted widely within the university and externally among its many collaborators. Industry suggested that much of their research work was interdisciplinary and often the interesting applied research was at the interfaces between traditional mono-disciplines. The university should consider ways in which an environment could be created which encouraged such interdisciplinary work. The business community also wanted a simplified method of access to the research knowledge within the university. Similar pressures came from within the university itself and it was realized that a major restructuring was required. After much further consultation the concept emerged of the creation of six multidisciplinary research institutes and a graduate school managed through a research and graduate college. All research and postgraduate activity would be managed through this college leaving departments to focus on teaching. However, as most staff contributed to both teaching and research a matrix style management structure was required for the university as a whole. Departments would still be the employer of a member of staff but each individual would look to departments for her or his teaching responsibilities and to the research institutes for their research effort. Funding was split between the two activities, with suitable safeguards for employment, so that the university could clearly identify and manage each activity.

A shift in the structure of this nature has significant repercussions for a member of staff including a change of allegiance for at least part of his or her university activity from department to research institute. It also has implications for the university's internal funding models and organization. It is still too soon to be able to judge such a change in its entirety but there is clear evidence of success and the active researchers have found it worthwhile. It has begun to break down the discipline barriers across the institution, not only within the research institutes themselves but across research institutes. For example, an environmental forum encompassing researchers from all research institutes has been formed to deal with multidisciplinary environmental research issues. Others are likely to be formed in IT and possibly health. By breaking the mould, freedom for innovation has been created.

Industry has welcomed the move and is beginning to work within the exciting and interesting new relationships being created. Entry into the university for research knowledge is now easier through each research institute's administration, and it is easier to bring appropriate multidiscipline teams together. It is taking time, but a key feature has been the awareness between staff of common methodologies and interests across disciplines which has proved particularly valuable. New professorial appointments are underway, some sponsored externally, which encourage and foster the new environment. This pioneering approach will take some years to reach its full potential but some success can be seen in the fact that according to the *Times Higher Education Supplement,* Salford had the highest climb in *The Times* 'League Table of Excellence for Research' of all the old University

Funding Council institutions in the 1996 research assessment exercise (THES 20 December 1996 (supplement)).

The CAMPUS organization remains active and a key player in university policy and contact with the business world. Its value can be seen in the commitment shown by key industrialists and its influence on the North-West region of England. It continues to provide support for the university research effort and brings together industrial groups to discuss key university topics. It is highly valued by those inside and outside the university.

Infrastructure and networking

There is yet another dimension to a university's links with industry which is relatively new and which was not part of the thinking of the 1980s. The growth of the Internet and the new superhighways has required a rethinking of a university's relationship to the community it serves. The traditional pattern of the full-time scholar attending for three or four years before returning to the 'outside world' has been steadily eroded over the past 20 years. Multi-mode courses, reductions in student grants and increased pressure to link courses with employment have all played their part. The new information channels will offer new opportunities for diversity of both input and output of knowledge. In addition the environment for learning may shift from the physical presence of the university to the workplace or to the home. (The success of the Open University for home learning suggests that the demand is there and that the supply side can provide the right material.) At the same time the linking together of organizations through the new fibre links will encourage new collaborations and juxtapositions which in themselves will encourage innovation. These networks will grow and will be oblivious of regions, states or even countries and it is probable that a world culture in education will develop. Some are forecasting that knowledge will be the main industry of the twenty-first century. Everyone wants it and soon it will be economic for everyone to get it. Within the current university system the leading research groups are almost always linked to other leading groups around the world. If they are not then their knowledge becomes marginalized. No longer can the full spectrum of knowledge be held by one group in one location, particularly when the knowledge is of an interdisciplinary nature. It applies equally from business to business, business to university as well as university to university. However, at the present time nobody quite knows how this will develop or what are the implications for the learning process – although there is much speculation! For a university devising its strategy for the next decade and beyond the information infrastructure and the networks they create cannot be ignored.

At Salford, and particularly within the Research and Graduate College, these issues have been at the forefront of strategy for the past four years. It was felt that in the medium and long term the new technologies would have a major impact on how the university linked with industry and its community, not only locally but worldwide. It became a deliberate policy, therefore, to seek opportunities which would ensure that the university was at the leading edge of the 'use' of the superhighways and that it could provide the best possible new services to the community which emerged through this advancement. In a chapter of this nature and length it would be impossible to cover all the initiatives that have been taken. However, they have resulted in over £20 million of investment from various funding sources and some key multidisciplinary research centres providing national and international focus. Some examples may give an indication but it should be realized that there is a coherence among all the initiatives and the aim is to provide the best service possible to all the communities the university serves.

A key initiative has been the GEMISIS programme (standing for 'government, education, medical, industrial and social information superhighway'). It has three main partners, Salford City Council (who have always been tremendous supporters of the university), NYNEX CableComms (another great supporter and now part of Cable and Wireless) and the university. The funding sources are varied and include the partners, the European Union (EU), the Training and Enterprise Council (TEC) and several organizations and businesses. It has involved the cabling of the whole of the university, including student bedrooms, and links out into the local community through the NYNEX cable company and internationally through the NYNEX FLAG (fibre link around the globe) project. The network created is now being used as a laboratory for the development of the superhighway which is attracting international interest. There are many interesting features to this multi-million pound project, including a virtual chamber of commerce linking the existing Manchester chamber to the university (by the end of 1998 1000 firms will have been connected); examination of telemedicine and security enhancement through use of the technology; linkage to schools to stimulate interest in learning and exchange; and over 35 doctoral students studying the use of the superhighway. When these projects report in three years' time it should be possible to assess more clearly the way ahead for the new technologies from a user perspective.

Another network has been created for a particular industry sector, that of construction. This is one of the largest industries in the world and Salford has one of the strongest international teams of researchers in IT and management applied to this industry. This strength has provided the opportunity to create a national network for the UK, supported by the Department of the Environment, to provide an industry-wide focus for the technology. Called CONSTRUCT IT, it brings together the leading contractors, clients, suppliers, consultants and computer/communication firms related to the industry for mutual benefit. Although inaugurated through the university it is led by industry and engages seven other universities (selected by the industry) to take the technology forward. It has begun to benchmark performance across firms, provide high-level courses (including an Engineering and Physical Science Research Council (EPSRC) integrated graduate development scheme), coordinate and encourage research and provide a technology showcase to assist investment by the industry. The model has now been adopted by organizations in nine countries and several others would like to join what is now becoming an 'international network of excellence'. Supported by the superhighway links, this virtual organization is taking the Salford masters degree in IT out to the Far East and several other areas. Its success is based on the confidence and trust built up over many years by the universities, and particularly Salford, with the industrial community in this sector.

More recently the university has invested in a new national industrial centre for virtual environments and has obtained government millennium funding for a new building in the heart of Manchester's business community at Salford Quays (the redeveloped area across Manchester's old dockland). It will involve a research and education centre specifically geared to industry developing the use of virtual worlds and visualization technologies. In addition there will be an interpretative centre, exhibition space for firms, education for school children and retail facilities all related to virtual reality and associated environments. It will be linked to the GEMISIS projects and the IT Institute. Like these other projects industry will be involved in leading and steering the research work. The new centre will, by its placement and organization, be at the very heart of the business community addressing that community's needs. In another domain the university is a partner alongside the other three universities in Manchester in the Business and Ecology Centre set up by the Cooperative Bank to provide specialist advice on the environment to organizations and particularly small and medium sized enterprises. Again, the superhighway infrastructure will be used to access firms and provide the knowledge in new and innovative ways. The siting of the centre on the Salford campus has helped the university link-in with its own environmental network group and it is anticipated that this will be of mutual benefit for many years to come.

Behind all these exemplars is an ethos which says that it is part of Salford's mission to be engaged with the community and in particular with industry and commerce. Again, the university is seeking new and innovative ways in which to cement that relationship and build on its existing strengths. In these cases, however, it is extending beyond its own boundary, linking with other universities and providing a platform in which all can grow together. It is not yet clear what the direction will be as industry itself changes in the light of the information revolution but what is clear is that the educational organizations must form a partnership with industry for both to reap the benefits.

Conclusions

The outline above has of necessity been a summary of the University of Salford's developing partnership with industry and the other communities it seeks to serve. Increasingly, as information technologies break down the

138 *Peter Brandon*

Figure 9.1 The axes of a research based university

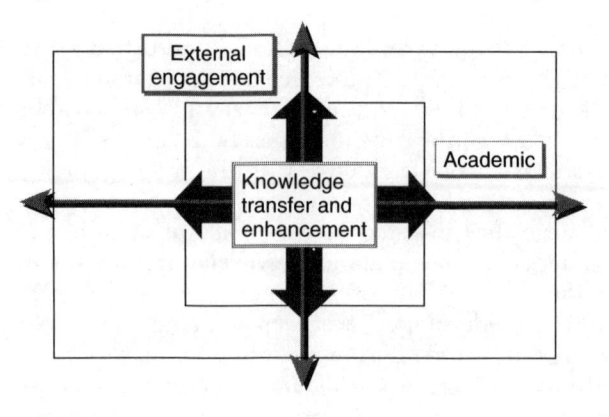

Figure 9.2 The prioritized axes

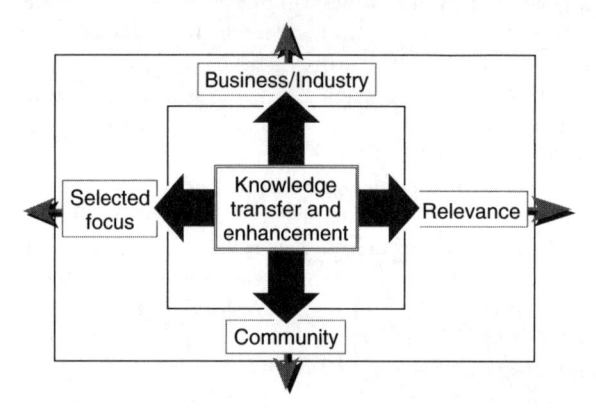

barriers between home, workplace and university, there will be a greater harmony between all three. Salford is now well placed to play an active part in the new environment.

The ethos has involved a recognition that for Salford, at least, there are two axes to its activity. At the heart of the university is its conventional mission to provide for knowledge transfer and enhancement. Across this mission is overlaid the two axes of academic development and external engagement as shown in Figure 9.1. In all university planning these two axes are considered and there is an imperative to include these on the agenda for the future. Extending Figure 9.1 further, the university has chosen to address the two axes by prioritizing as shown in Figure 9.2.

The external engagement axis is clear but in Salford's case on the academic axis it has chosen to concentrate on relevance and a deliberate focus on those issues which will aid business, industry and the community. This can be taken a stage further to provide the framework for the university core

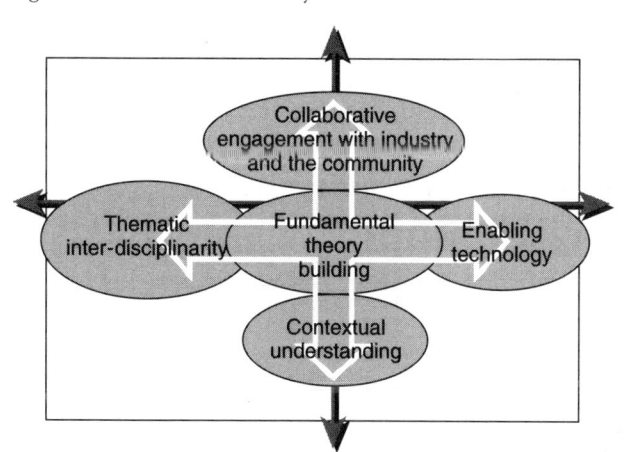

Figure 9.3 Salford University's vision for research

[Figure: Diagram showing five interconnected ovals with arrows. Central oval "Fundamental theory building" connects to "Collaborative engagement with industry and the community" (top), "Thematic inter-disciplinarity" (left), "Enabling technology" (right), and "Contextual understanding" (bottom).]

activities. For example, the Salford vision for research could be shown as demonstrated in Figure 9.3.

These in turn can be translated into how each research institute would respond under this framework for its particular research communities. It provides a rich picture of the university within an ethos which is consistent and well-founded, leading to an important partnership with external agencies.

Looking back, it is possible to distinguish key issues which have resulted in the strengthening of the partnership. While it is not perfect and still evolving these issues are central to the success which Salford enjoys and may contain lessons for others. The following list gives the major issues but it should be recognized that it is the gathering together of many strands, creating confidence with business and a willingness to change to suit industry's needs that has allowed the bridge between academia and industry to be made. The whole is more than the sum of the parts.

- A long-standing commitment to applied research and education for capability.
- A willingness to change and adapt to new circumstances.
- Strong leadership with a vision which encompasses the concept of partnership.
- A commitment by the body of academics and university council to the concept of partnership.
- Intelligence of both sectors, academe and business.
- An external context which encourages collaboration.
- Champions at a high-level in industry and government willing to help.
- An organization with status in the university organization (such as CAMPUS) to aid leadership, strategy and policy making.
- A university management willing to cut through unnecessary constraints.
- A mechanism for two-way communication to build confidence.

- An infrastructure which is flexible to address change brought about by new technology.
- A mechanism for taking applied research and development out into the market-place.
- A vision which extends into the future beyond just local requirements and a framework within which it can develop.

Some of the initiatives mentioned in this chapter are only just beginning and it is too early to describe their impact. Nevertheless, the signs are good and there is little doubt that the strong industrial partnership Salford built in the early 1980s will continue for some time to come.

Acknowledgements

The author wishes to acknowledge the very valuable help provided by Stuart Bosworth, registrar for much of the period described, and Lorraine Baric, pro-vice-chancellor in the early 1980s. They provided insights into the historical relationship with business at Salford but the views expressed are those of the author alone.

References

Ashworth, J. (1985) Universities and industry: national and institutional perspectives. *Oxford Review of Education*, II (3), 225–43.
Deas, I., Robson, B., Topham, N. and Twomey, J. (1995) *The Impacts of Greater Manchester's Universities*, Summary Overview (p. 5), Manchester, University of Manchester.
HMSO (1993) *Realising Our Potential*, government White Paper on research policy. London, HMSO.
NCIHE (National Committee of Enquiry into Higher Education) (1997) *Report of the Committee of Enquiry into the Funding of Higher Education* (the Dearing Report). London, DfEE.
Hutton, W. (1996) *The State We're In*. London, Vintage.
University of Salford, Senate Minutes (1992) Minutes of November 1992 (internal document).

10

The University of Sheffield's Regional Office: Forging Relationships Between a Traditional Civic University and its Regional Community

Marilyn Wedgwood and Brigitte Pemberton

Sheffield is in an area which has traditionally been dependent on the coal and steel industries. In common with many cities throughout Europe, Sheffield has experienced industrial decline, primarily as a consequence of pit closures and the steel industry's reduced dependency on manpower. As a consequence, the city and the region is undergoing a process of regeneration and revitalization. The university, with its huge resources and its wide-ranging expertise has much to bring to this process.

It has not been a habit for the city or the region to seek expert help from the university or for the university to engage in a significant way with the city and the region in its work. In short, the university's expertise was not fully recognized or understood and it had not been properly harnessed for the city's and region's development. While some of the research carried out was done with companies and organizations in the region, the university was mainly in the business of basic research and operated in an international community, being less concerned with the direct application of new ideas and technology to business and industrial problems. The challenge was to manage a change process – to bring different cultures together.

Professor Gareth Roberts came to the university in 1991 as its new vice-chancellor. He understood only too well the impact the university can and does make on the local economy. Not only because it is a major employer (the third largest in Sheffield), but also because of the wide-ranging expertise of the staff and the students. He led the university into a new and stronger relationship with the regional community.

The approach that was adopted was threefold:

1. In the first instance, the university established a regional strategy as part of its corporate plan and made explicit its commitment to the region. This was backed up with resources and staff.
2. In the second case, the vice-chancellor began to build strong relationships and alliances with key players from the public and private sector in the city and the region, in formal and informal ways. Over the past ten years, Sheffield has established a tradition for developing regeneration strategies which are owned, developed and implemented by the major players in the city, including the university. This partnership approach recognized that the future success of the city required an awareness of the interdependence of the major organizations and the city administration. The vice-chancellor is a leading member of key partnership groups. He ensured that the university was active in new developments.
3. The third part of his approach was to provide a clear contact point, and in 1993 the university established its regional office. In essence, it provided the 'one-stop shop' to make access to the university much easier. The establishment of the regional office was an unequivocal statement to the region that the university was committed. It was set up on a non-commercial basis to encourage partnerships and interaction, and this is reflected in its mission statement: 'To encourage an enhanced interchange between the University and the Region, so that Sheffield and its Region capitalise on the University's intellectual resources and, in turn, the University draws on the resources and expertise of the Region in its research and teaching'.

The regional office therefore, became the focal point for the interactions between the university and the city and its surrounding region, dealing with enquiries, bringing people together, developing and administering new schemes and programmes, liaising extensively and in different ways with all sectors of the community, and representing the university at functions and events. (The main schemes are briefly outlined in the sections that follow and align with the five strategic objectives of the regional office.)

These steps provided the systematic approach that was needed to bring about cultural change, both within the university and within the local community. There are tangible results which continue to grow.

The university has become a significant player in programmes of social and economic regeneration. Not only has it contributed to the development of the plans, it is also committed to the implementation of those plans. New schemes have evolved, led by the university, to bring university staff and students into working contact with the regional community, and there is a wider network of contacts and a stronger university presence in the community. Some of these have attracted major financial support from projects such as the European Regional Development Fund.

The University of Sheffield's regional strategy is now developing along five major fronts, which add to and complement the normal range of activities followed by a university in 'town and gown' links. All five fronts are now discussed in turn.

The establishment of strategic links with key groups and organizations concerned with city and regional development

The university has become a key player in economic and social development plans for the city, with specific responsibilities in local plans. Alliances are now well established with key agencies concerned with regional economic development and growth such as the Training and Enterprise Council (TEC), the city council, business links, the regional government offices, and the university is an active member of the Yorkshire and Humber University Association.

The establishment of schemes and initiatives which provide for 'low barrier' ways of working with the university

One example of this approach is the PLUS scheme. PLUS stands for Project Link University of Sheffield, and builds on a normal part of our work in the university. Most final-year students and postgraduates undertake a project, thesis or dissertation as an assessed part of their course. This project or dissertation must meet all the rigours of academe, and satisfy the examiners. However, much of the work that the students undertake does, or could, have direct relevance to an organization external to the university, and our aim is to make this expertise easily available by bringing the students and the external organization together in project work.

The target was to involve 20 per cent of the eligible students in 1996. Over 2000 students were involved in the scheme across 43 departments in the university, and involvement was with all sectors of the community: business, industry, commerce, public sector and community and voluntary organizations. This initiative provides on average 600 person years from the university to local businesses and organizations. The work that the students undertake adds value to their courses. They have the opportunity to gain practical skills and business experience, which clearly helps in strengthening the employability of university graduates.

The regional office manages the scheme and therefore the organization only has to make contact with one office in the first instance. We have a code of practice in operation and give support, guidance and training where appropriate.

PLUS SME (PLUS for small and medium sized enterprises) was set up as a very focused initiative. The most important impact of PLUS SME in the context of this chapter is that it gave access to the university's expertise in a simple and non-threatening way, with minimal resources or financial contributions by the organization. Sixty per cent of companies continue their relationship with the university through the PLUS SME scheme, taking on graduates on a regular basis. Twenty-five per cent of the PLUS SME projects are referred to other university technology transfer projects such as Medilink, Environet, the Centre for Corrosion Technology and the Waste Management and Technology Centre. PLUS therefore helps to raise awareness of the university as a resource for the region, and it also raises awareness of the region as a resource for the university in research and teaching.

Because of the simplicity of the relationship, it helps to dispel misconceptions and build trust, and this in turn paves the way for continuing involvement. Businesses and other organizations are more receptive to the idea of working with the university and continue those links in a variety of ways using, for example, subsidized schemes and sponsorship of postgraduates. Equally, the university staff maintain contacts with the businesses and the organizations to enhance their research and enrich their teaching. In short, PLUS and PLUS SME are helping in the process of cultural change, and other cities and universities in the UK have followed this lead.

Formed in 1987, the Managing Directors Club with a membership of over 100, drawn from many of the region's leading companies, meets throughout the year for informal dinners with guest speakers. The explicit aim of the club is to create an effective venue which encourages the exchange of information and expertise between the university and companies in the region. By meeting on a regular basis, with a stimulus provided by a keynote address given by a senior figure from government, industry or commerce, common interests can be explored further and networks expanded. Similar clubs exist for other network groups, such as the Green Business Club or the Schools and Colleges, University Club.

The initiation and development of business sector networks which match onto the university's research expertise in sectors with the potential to grow

This approach builds on the university's research expertise. We have begun to identify where the university's research strengths match the business sectors which are important for the region's growth and development. These may be existing major sectors or those sectors with the potential to grow. Our approach is to engage businesses of different sizes from the SMEs to the multinationals.

Currently, we have identified three major areas where the matching obviously occurs:

1. Materials and engineering materials. The programmes which are developing are the Materials Forum and the Materials Technopole.

2. The medical technology, health and health-related sector. The programme emerging here is Medilink.
3. The environmental industries sector, where the evolving scheme is Environet (now called EBN – the Environmental Business Network). Its objective is to support business development and market effectiveness in the environmental industries sector within Yorkshire and the Humber, focusing on products and services that minimize negative impact on the environment.

The schemes in each of these sectors are evolving slightly differently, but the principle remains the same. The university is committed to helping these sectors grow by focusing research on their needs for product and process development and by aiding the training and updating of skills. We are working closely with the government office of the Yorkshire and Humber region to fit in with and influence their strategic plans, in particular within the regional innovation strategy, which is developing along business-sector lines. The following examples illustrate the slightly different approaches.

The Materials Forum

The Materials Forum is coordinated by one of a group of experienced industrialists who have been appointed to the university as industrial advisers. Ten of the major steel companies in the area (combined annual turnover: £1.5 billion) have been brought together to undertake research and development work arising directly from their business needs. Each company pays a subscription, which provides scholarships for postgraduate students and a salary for a research fellow. A project working-group led by one of the industrialists identifies the projects that clusters of companies are interested in. At the current time, we have 30 collaborative research and development projects underway and a number of masters projects. In addition the members receive technical reports and a programme of informal seminars on technical issues important to their industry.

Sharing information with each other has resulted in cross-fertilization of ideas which advances the competitiveness of the business. The Forum is emerging as a valuable tool to focus academic sights on the technology support needs of Sheffield's materials industry. The link between research and industry is highly focused and woven into the Foresight aspirations. The Materials Forum has been running for two years and has already been used to lever-in additional funds to enhance the research activity for the Forum members. In addition, the businesses are building links with other parts of the university in, for example, quality management and environmental management. The Materials Forum is a prestigious club for leading-edge materials processing companies, primarily designed for the larger companies.

The university is also an active partner in the Materials Technopole, which provides technology transfer and general specialist support to SMEs.

Medilink

Medilink is a network primarily for SMEs in the region. It has been set up to support the medical technology companies across Yorkshire and the Humber region, and has evolved into a professional association. It brings together universities, medical technology companies, their customers (the hospitals) and the business support agencies in four areas of activity: product development, training and updating, marketing and exporting, and intelligence and information flow. It aims to increase the competitiveness of the medical technology sector.

The development of the network was built on a series of events to bring the different parties together. The first National Orthopaedic Conference (Ortho '96) for example, involved 200 attendees and resulted in significant business opportunities for 20 local companies. A product innovation centre has been established with a strong customer-orientated approach. Since its launch in September 1996 the team has handled over 50 new or improved medical product opportunities. The businesses are benefiting: 1500 receive a newsletter raising awareness of key issues, new product opportunities are identified and taken forward, training on, for example, CE marking is provided and marketing and sales are improved through trade fares and exhibitions. This project, which receives substantial support from the European Regional Development Fund, has become a model for organizing other sector/university linked initiatives. Medilink itself has grown from a regional initiative to a national network.

The promotion of educational access and attainment within local communities

The city and the region is concerned about raising educational attainment at all levels. After-school participation in education is well below the UK average. The university, while obviously providing education, embarked on a series of activities to raise educational aspirations and to provide access to higher education (HE) in general through the Sheffield University Network for Education in the Community. The programme is primarily aimed at the non-traditional student – that is, those that do not fit the normal entry requirement. The Early Outreach programme was launched in 1992, involving parents, teachers and pupils. Residential weekends, visits, parent evenings, curriculum-based activities and student tutoring combine to develop positive attitudes to educational attainment. Compacts with local colleges and schools focus on students who have the potential to succeed in HE but are not ordinarily considering it as an option. Students from socio-economic groups who are underrepresented in HE are made an early offer of a place at the university in order to increase their confidence and motivate them to continue their studies. The Dearne College is an exciting new initiative in a mining community within the region which will deliver HE through telematics learning. The Department of Adult Continuing Education provides a comprehensive programme of over 900 courses covering a range of subjects enabling people all over the region to study for qualifications offered by the university. In addition, the university is involved with strategic alliances and partnerships operating across the city and the region, to give coherence to a range of initiatives aimed at raising educational attainment.

The embedding of the research capability of the university into the work of the regional community

Many different activities and approaches are operating, targeted at individual academics, departments and externals, across all disciplines and sectors. The essential element is collaboration – working together from different perspectives to a common goal. External organizations are becoming involved in different ways with the core research activity of the university, which adds to the usual and expanding commercial consultancy activities, and more researchers from all disciplines are looking to the region as a research field, developing liaisons in which they apply their researching expertise within the context of local issues.

Various activities are underway. The Institute of Work Psychology, for example, conducts its research on the impact of technological change on work performance, with local organizations and businesses. Social scientists are engaged in research work on ethnic issues with the local police, and others are working with the local authorities to help evaluate new programmes concerned with community development or advise on housing and transport policy. Heating the city through waste incineration was a concept developed by the university for the city and led to the establishment of Sheffield Heat and Power. Sheffield has become Britain's leading authority on waste incineration providing advice to most of the major incineration plants in the country by maintaining close working relations with the researchers at the university. Many scientists and engineers in the university are linked with local business on research and development, which is improving products and processes to maintain a competitive edge.

Reflections on the process

Perhaps what is most important in this whole process, a process of change, is that the university is taking the lead. It is proactive in identifying and clarifying where and how it can have some impact, and in working out and testing the best ways of doing so, in a way which is consistent with its own mission, and beneficial to those outside. The regional office, with its specific brief to interact with the region, has a pivotal role to play in this process.

But the road is not easy. There are, of course, difficulties, and these seem to fall into four main categories:

1. Time: because we are trying to effect a cultural change on both sides of the divide. It takes time to change attitudes and practices and to gain trust and understanding. It takes time to face up to the prejudice, fear and hostility that occurs during the process. We handle this by encouraging engagement across all sectors with all parts of the university and by being persistent and consistent in the messages that we give.
2. Cultural differences: as the engagement continues, we become increasingly aware of the cultural differences, both their degree and nature, such as language, dress, and operational and management styles. The approach we take is to recognize these, identify them and be able to articulate the similarities and the differences. We then apply and use this understanding to build partnerships and relationships, not only by drawing attention to them, but also by identifying how these differences complement each other to bring benefits to both sides.
3. Lack of understanding about the nature of university research: it has become increasingly apparent that businesses, whether they come from the public or private sector, are used to working with external experts through a process of consultancy in which they define the problem and engage the consultants to address it. Within a traditional civic university, like the University of Sheffield, researchers are driven by a thirst for knowledge and in consequence, they challenge the existing status quo to take ideas forward. Engagement with a partner outside would therefore have to provide some stimulus within this context. The university does, of course, engage in commercial consultancy, but even within this process many academics won't give it a high priority unless it gives them an opportunity to further their own research, particularly in the current time in the UK where publication of research in an international context is crucial. We seek to raise awareness of this process and to encourage partnership and collaboration in research as distinct from formal consultancy.
4. Academics' concerns about diluting scholarship: on the contrary side, the academics themselves have concerns that working with live problems dilutes scholarship. Though this may sometimes be the case, there are circumstances in which collaboration with partners outside creates new ideas, new issues, new problems and new contexts for research which are legitimate within academe. Student projects themselves and the informal processes of getting people to meet and talk do much to address this particular difficulty.

In summary, the way we face up to these difficulties and make the city/university relationship work, is to stimulate engagement but to manage it carefully, to be persistent, to maintain contacts and continuity. We recognize and celebrate the complementary nature of the differences, and we are patient.

The benefits to the university are clear. The research process has become more iterative as researchers work more closely with the public, industrial and commercial sectors. Researchers have been given greater access to resources in the community to help them test out the findings of their research and in many cases have been able to make use of a wider source of testing equipment, technical facilities and data and information sources. The research in social policy subjects has, due to increased collaboration with public sector professionals, influenced local and regional policy. All this has been achieved because the focus of the collaboration has been 'coincidence of interest' and the university's objective to develop its research excellence has not been compromised.

Conclusion

This chapter has provided an indication of the approach that we are taking. The university is committed; the regional office has a pivotal role in the process. It is the office in the university that has the specific brief to link with the region and therefore to build up relationships and partnerships. The university gains and the city and region gain. Together we are learning how to unlock the complementary expertise resources for mutual benefit.

Since the inception of the regional office in 1992, the world has changed. The Research Assessment Exercise (RAE), Teaching Quality Assessment (TQA), a new government, regionalism and Regional Development Agencies and the Dearing Report continue to provide a challenge to us.

Through small steps and large ones, we are experiencing a stronger interaction between the university and the regional community. The university is addressing seriously its role in regional competitiveness and generating creative ways of working which are consistent with the core business of teaching and research. Increasingly, as we listen to the external organizations, we are focusing on and targeting activities that really add value and bring mutual benefits. The university and the business community are each learning and shifting to make engagement successful.

The challenge is to link exploitation and knowledge transfer to the core work of the university's research and teaching quality, assessed by the RAE and TQA respectively.

The university, through its regional strategy, is being creative in transferring its excellence in teaching and research to the community and the region. It does this in a context in which positive exploitation of the knowledge base for economic benefit and competitiveness is not defined as core responsibility for universities, either in the funding allocation or assessments. However, it is obvious that the tremendous knowledge and expertise needs to be tapped for the economic and social well-being of the country.

11

Towards the Community University

Harry Gray

Fresh thoughts

It was only after I had put this collection together that I realized that there was a missing element describing clearly how universities might change beyond the incremental changes that they are undergoing. I had the privilege to be in on some of the early thinking about the University of Cumbria following on from a suggestion by Dale Campbell-Savours that there was a good case for a University of the Lakes (Campbell-Savours 1995). The idea of a new university in a new location was not new, the most recent being the University of the Highlands, and so the small team considering the strategic concepts and what the vision might be were able to start not entirely from scratch but with some knowledge of what others were also thinking and trying to do. What follows is largely the substance of my original position paper in which I was less concerned with producing a research paper than reflecting the thoughts that many of us had shared with one another over a period of some months.

The starting point for our thinking was to understand what justification there was for a new university. The original key surmise was that more school-leavers should be encouraged to go to university and if they could not go away, then they could attend one locally. But our justification was different, though not unrelated. The reason for a new university for Cumbria was basically economic. We wanted to improve not just the skill levels of young and old workers in the county but the general level of economic capacity and capability. We wanted to help in the development of a world-class economic community based on indigenous industries that were capable of being sustained from within the resource base of the county and not dependent on incoming leadership or control. We wanted to help to build a self-sustaining economic foundation which would be based on the contributions of everyone in the county of all ages. It would in fact not be a university for the traditional and selected favoured few but a university for everyone irrespective of their academic starting point. As an idea it goes far beyond anything that most university people were thinking about at the time but it has appeal to many academics who favour higher education (HE) as a democratic service.

The changing scene of HE

All British universities are in the midst of a period of rapid and fundamental organizational change, the consequences of which have yet to be determined. One thing universities can never be accused of is systematic planning and most changes are incremental, gradual and piecemeal. Nevertheless the changes are significant to such an extent that universities may be changing their character altogether. Certainly universities are becoming more aware of pressures to engage in work-related activity, to be more concerned with economic generation and more applied in their research. But there is a limit as to how much change and adaptation they can undergo before they fall apart, disintegrating as teaching, research and consultancy separate out into distinctly organized functions increasingly unrelated to one another.

There is a tension between universities being concerned with academic and long-term matters of intellectual development and a concern with immediate and applied learning and investigation. Clearly the polytechnic experiment in the UK whereby there was the pure and applied distinction between institutions was seen to have failed when all institutions became universities and academic drift was consolidated. The HE colleges that remained have tried to ease their way into the university sector (choosing titles such as 'a university-sector institution') so it is perhaps necessary to invent a new kind of university. There is little likelihood that universities as we have known them will continue as such if their intake increases beyond 40 per cent of the age group yet it should be possible to offer 80 per cent – or even more – of the population the benefits of HE if a different model of learning and assessing achievement were invented. If one sees universities as being in a position to offer their intellectual capital to the world rather than having to collect the most biddable people into them in order to maintain their intellectual stock it is possible to conceive of HE quite differently. This becomes possible by developing the idea of the 'community university', a real university (with some 'virtual' characteristics) existing in parallel with the traditional university but separate from it in values and organization.

A community perspective

It is easier to conceptualize the idea of a community university in geographical form, though topographical isolation is not a necessary condition. Cumbria is the best example after Cornwall of a separated geographical entity in England and it has never had a university situated within its boundaries (nor has Shropshire and the concept can be applied there, too). Some universities outside the county have set up enclaves but these locations are extensions of the parent institution and do not spring out of the locality nor respond to local needs. These incursive operations are not so much concerned with the development of the local community, but are rather reinforcements of the parent institution's resources and status. They tend to draw students away from the county as they are a means of egress to the world outside with its opportunities for employment and further study. They are part of the social mobility function of universities and somewhat unsympathetic to students who may wish to live in their home surroundings rather than find work further afield or abroad.

A community university would be concerned with enriching the life of the whole community through general access to HE at a neighbourhood level. Its purpose would not be to help people to leave the locality but to bring new industries and businesses and a richer cultural life into each neighbourhood. A community university would encourage people to look outside to discover what is good and worthwhile, but instead of having to move away in order to enjoy them, the benefits would be made available locally. In fact the basic economic problem of Cumbria and Cornwall is that there is not a high enough level of wealth-creating skills within each county for the people who live there. But if there were, most localities in Cumbria would be as good as anywhere in the world to live. A university focused on the geographical area of the county would be the prime generator of economic development bringing social and cultural enrichment into the community and generating social energy for self-renewal and a self-sustaining economy.

Organization and structure

Even the Open University and the University of the Highlands and Islands do not have the characteristics of a true community university because they deliver mainly pre-packaged programmes into the locality that have been developed outside on criteria of supposed general applicability. Perhaps the geography of western Scotland is not hospitable enough for the richest forms of community life (though the Gaelic College has much to offer in particular cultural settings). A true community approach would build on what is there and produce bespoke programmes of local application. Many of the so-called new university institutions simply offer distance learning in the same way as conventional university programmes. They might use the latest electronic telematic equipment but they do so in conventional ways to assist learning of a traditional kind. Much adult education – particularly the kind traditionally offered by Ruskin and Northern College – is very conservative and old-fashioned in its approach, aimed at bringing Oxbridge education to the underprivileged through lectures and instruction. A community university requires a different view of learning, as of knowledge and information; and the modes of learning that inform its processes have to be of a quite different nature from those that imbue élitist organizations. It also has close interaction with the other social and economic activities of the region and draws on the culture that is there as well as national and international resources.

The traditional view of HE is that it involves the transmission of knowledge and opinions that are valued by the educated élite to those who wish to be inducted into the scholastic brotherhood. It is driven by the suppliers because it is the lecturers who decide what should be learned and how it should be valued. The community university on the contrary is consumer driven; it is the learners who decide what they want to learn and how it should be evaluated. Of course, the polarity is less stark in practice than it sounds and many modern approaches to learning are much more based on mutuality and equality. But most university activity and basic thinking is predicated on the idea that university academics are ahead of their lay colleagues and the direction of knowledge dissemination is one-way. Certainly that is the basis of most undergraduate education and course structure. There are comparatively few (but perhaps an increasing number) of programmes based on student-centred learning and involving exploration and discovery approaches, but even these can be authoritarian.

Content and process

The community university is based not on the content of learning – that is, what should be remembered and how it should be understood – but on the process of learning; that is, how the learner manages the process of learning and evaluates it. The raw data or knowledge may be the same but the context is different. The traditional university values data in the context of received academic opinion whereas the learner-centred process values data for the applications the learner determines for it. If a student takes a university degree, obtaining that degree admits them to a privileged group which has a measure of separation from ordinary life – the academic community. Having a university degree places the graduate in a special position outside the normal home group. In the demotic community model of learning, what the individual learns has primary relevance in the community in which the learners live and work. Instead of taking learners out of their home situation it enhances the quality of that situation and benefits the learners, their families and their colleagues.

For most people the value of learning is the value it gives to the quality of life – the individual's social and economic milieu. The learning by the individual enriches the life of the community and collective learning builds stronger cultural and working resourcefulness as each member of the community shares their learning. Learning individuals help to build learning groups and learning groups compose learning organizations and whole learning communities. The fact that universities are organized on a traditional and essentially élitist selective and exclusive model means that learning is an inwardly directed, personally exclusive activity rather than an outwardly directed socially shared one. If there is to be any socially useful derivative from personal learning then there must be a new form of structure for the university; this is the community model discussed in outline here.

The community model

The community model is based on the idea that learning takes its meaning from the social contexts in which it first occurs and is later applied. This will often mean the economic circumstances of individuals – their place of work – but it may also mean their social, personal and private life. The motivation to learn comes from the individual as a natural aspect of their natural curiosity and ambition. It is the sense of self-esteem driving people to wish to achieve that is the spur to learning. The bottom line of assessment and evaluation is the opinion and judgement of the individual learner though the processes are not performed in isolation but with reference to valued peers or significant others. The basis of assessment is the usefulness to the learner not the preference of the teacher. Therefore a community university is structured around the drive to learn of individuals who manage their own learning programmes but with the assistance of helpers – both those who help with the learning process (facilitators) and those who help with exposition and explanation (teachers). For all learners their domestic situation will be the key location that gives meaning to what they learn. The workplace will determine the starting point for occupational and vocational advancement while family needs and interests will determine the kind of things people want to learn about for personal reasons. There will be many partners in such learning – friends, family members, employers, customers, and valued or significant others at the perimeter of current life experience.

Formal structures

The formal role of the community university is to provide support for the learning process, ensure that standards are achieved and that credit is awarded appropriately for achievement. The conventional terminology of units, certificates, diplomas and degrees can be used because the programmes accumulate *pari passu* with equivalence to a traditional university – otherwise the community learning programme would not be a 'university' programme. But the concept of university means depth and progression for the individual, not admission to a select coterie. The University of Cumbria will be organized around a credit framework that recognizes achievement and ambition but will allow individuals to grow through transformation rather than by linear rote-memory.

Organizationally, the community university provides a simple credit framework that embraces all possible ways of learning (not just formally delivered and assessed lecture courses). The credit units can be achieved in a very wide range of ways – portfolios, records of achievement, tests and examinations, assessment of prior learning, formal credit units, self-managed programmes of study or investigation, artefacts produced for work purposes and so on. Indeed, the academic programme of the community university draws on real life experiences at work and at home for its material and validated experiences. A report on a work-based problem may be the equivalent of a case study in a formal university course. A problem-solving task in actual employment is equivalent to a case study on a formally instructed management course. But learning is not solely by 'addition and accumulation' but by a variety of personal 'changes of state' whereby endogenous personal growth is recognized.

Students will for the most part study with other students but no two people will necessarily be following the same study pattern. Or if they are doing the same thing such as learning a foreign language they may each be aiming at a different level. Programmes will be run through a central administration whose key role is to service the needs of students. Rather than advertising courses and recruiting for them, students will decide on what they want both individually and collectively and appropriate assistance will be bought in. Some parts of an individual's programme will be in formal university situations but others will be in special learning groups. For most students the emphasis will be occupational and vocational needs and they will virtually all be home based. Some components will be parts of professional qualifications but some will be self-selected. Special locations will be established throughout the county where community learning will be possible and one of the most exciting opportunities is to design appropriate learning foyers for villages and small towns (Library Information Commission 1997). Nearly all formal learning will be based essentially on real life experience rather than contrived instructional drill.

Levels of achievement

On the 'Cumbria' model – although this part is still at the moment an abstraction at the stage of exemplary conceptualization – there will be three levels of 'university' achievement, each separately organized but articulated through the common credit framework. The first level starts at school and goes up to first degree level. The second level embraces a masters degree by independent learning with three equal components: knowledge, understanding and capability, in the occupational, vocational and personal domains. The third level will be research supported by a seminar and tutorial programme associated with a number of Cumbria institutes which develop an international study and research function based on the major industries in the county. Such institutes might include a Lakes Hotel School and a Lakes Institute for the Management of Area and Regional Economies (LIMARE), both of which are under active discussion. Students will be expected and required to organize and manage their own careers so as to accumulate experiences for appropriate assessment and these will be collected in a learning record or portfolio to provide evidence of achievement at key levels, probably stored on a 'smart card'.

A university system

A community university will be inexpensive to run compared with traditional universities since it is basically an administrative system which buys-in the necessary personnel to service student needs and requirements. As a region-wide system it has advantages over the single institution. For instance, the community university system would have some of its course graduates accredited by a variety of nearby universities but one leading institution to foster development in each academic area and extend the breadth of provision. The initial or baseline level is to be managed through the further education (FE) college sector with the support of schools and including normal school-leaving qualifications and sub-degree (e.g. Higher National Certificate (HNC)) work. Beyond graduate level is the masters level which is overseen by the 'lead' university through its learning institute and continuing education department (Continuing Vocational Education and Training (CVET)/Continuing Professional Development (CPD)). The third level is provided by the county institutes which are private companies that run world-class seminars in a range of areas of economic and social value to the community. All teaching staff will be trained in learning facilitation through the community university learning institute and have obtained appropriate qualifications. Specialist lecturing staff will be chosen from an international panel. Several overseas universities with known specialist competence will run courses specifically as summer schools in association with the community university system (CUS). Most programmes however will be run in association with employers or community associations and will arise out of identified needs in social or economic circumstances. The University for Industry (UfI) will be incorporated in appropriate programmes in that UfI activities can be credited within the award framework.

In essence a CUS is managed through an administrative unit that treats students as customers and provides appropriate learning opportunities directly or through market research. For programmes originating outside the system there is an enhanced service fee, while those originating within the system are made available at economic cost. Various additional income-generating activities support the system but the main charge on university funds – lecturing staff – is mitigated by hiring staff for specific purposes at a daily or task contract rate. The academic activity of the CUS is overseen by a board of regents that consists of a dozen academics of international standing as experts in adult learning and subject specialisms. As indicated earlier, learning locations with specially designed accommodation include FE colleges and schools within the county as well as purpose-built accommodation in other types of property.

Research

A community university has an interest in research but it is applied research and, where appropriate, blue skies investigation. But the provenance and application are important and distinctive. Because the institutes are based on local industrial and public service need, they are grounded in the activities of the community. The kind of problems they deal with are those of immediate concern to regional businesses and arise out of an identification of economic and social need. For example, if there were to be a food institute in Cumbria (possibly associated with the Lakes Hotel School) it would be concerned with the many problems of speciality food production, which is a growing part of the local small and medium sized enterprise (SME) business sector. But also in Cumbria there is British Nuclear Fuels (BNF) with its world reputation for nuclear engineering where research of the most advanced nature is undertaken. The problem with traditional universities is that they think of themselves as having to deliver 'world-class research' as if it existed in its own right and without attachment to local organizations. Yet even in Cambridge association between university and commercial production is driving the establishment of high technology locations. However, the primary consideration of the community university is the improvement of the quality of life for its local clients, and the best ways of doing this – whatever they are – will be used.

References

Campbell-Savours, D. (1995) *The Case for the University of the Lakes.* Worthington, West Cumbria Development Agency.

Library Information Commission (1997) *The New Library: The People's Network.* London, LIC.

Index

academic capital, 24–5
academic capitalism, 26, 32–3
academic development, 138
access, educational, 96–7, 118, 146–7
achievement, levels of, 155–6
administrative system, 156
adult education, 118, 147, 152
agriculture, 110
Akamatsu, K., 81
Amin, A., 39
animateurs, 45
applied research, 8, 11, 52–3, 133
Arts Centre, 119
ASEAN countries, 80–92
Ashworth, J., 125–6, 128, 129, 130
Asian economies, 30, 80–92
Asian values, 80, 83
assessment, 45
attainment, educational, 146–7
Australia, 20, 32
autonomy, universities and, 44

Bain, G., 116
Barro, R., 29
Bayoumi, T., 56
Bhattacharyya, K., 115
biological sciences, 110
Blair, T., 97, 120
Bolton Report, 66, 69
Boston, 31
Bosworth, S., 126
British Nuclear Fuels (BNF), 157
Browne, J., 117
Business and Ecology Centre, 137

business education, 87–8, 102, 110
business/industry
  developing intellectual capital, 15–16
  generic skills and competencies, 74–6
  marginal activity, 10
  marketing universities and regional development, 43–4
  partnerships, *see* collaboration
  SMEs, *see* small and medium sized enterprises
  spillover effect, 30–2
  universities and innovation, 26, 52–3
  University of Sheffield links with, 143–6
  University of Sunderland Industry Centre, 105–6
  University of Teesside and, 97–102
  University of Warwick and, 115–17, 119–20
business schools, 8, 10
  Warwick Business School, 116–17, 120
Butcher, J., 112
Butcher Report, 130
Butterworth, J., 110

Campbell-Savours, D., 150
CAMPUS (Campaign for the University of Salford), 128–9, 130, 135
CAMPUS Academic Venture and Enterprise (CAVE) fund, 129

Index 159

Canada, 6
  economic impact of universities, 47–65
capability, educating for, 126
Carlisle campus of University of Northumbria, 102–4
Castells, M., 28
causation, 55–7
change
  in HE sector, 3–4, 15–16, 151
  re-scoping the university, 12–15
  Salford University, 127–31, 132–3
  universities and economic change, 89–90
China, 30
choice, 11–12
  multiple choice, 42
Chowdhry, A., 81, 85
city development, 143
City of Sunderland Partnership, 105
civic engagement, networks of, 42
civic universities, 5
Cockman, R., 74–6
cognitive sunk costs, 32–3
collaboration, 12, 15, 44–5
  HE and SMEs, 76–9
  Salford University and industrial partnership, 123–40
  University of Sheffield and, 142, 143–6, 147–9
Colleges of Advanced Technology (CATs), 5
'colonies', Science Park, 114
Commission on National Investment in Higher Education, 21
Committee of Vice-chancellors and Principals (CVCP), 9
communication, 39
community
  impact of University of Warwick, 109–22
  North-East England universities and communities, 95–108
  see also local environment; regional development
Community Informatics Research Applications Unit (CIRA), 96–7
community model of learning, 154
community university, 150–7
community university system (CUS), 156

competence, 38–9
competitiveness, 97–101
Computervision, 116
concepts, 38–9
connections, 38–9
Constantine College, 95–6
  see also Teesside, University of
CONSTRUCT IT, 136–7
construction management course, 130
consultancy, 9, 15, 148
continuing education, 118, 147
corporate government, 90
county research institutes, 155, 156, 157
Coventry, 109–10, 112–13
Coventry College of Education, 117–18
Cranfield University, 8, 10
credit framework, 154–5
Crosland, A., 110, 111
cultural differences, 148
Cumbria, University of, 6, 13, 150–7
custom-designed degree courses, 10
customers/clients, relationships with, 10–13
  see also business/industry; collaboration

Dearing Report, 4, 20, 71, 77, 95, 132
  Knowledge House, 102
Dearne College, 146–7
Deas, I., 124
Department for Education and Employment (DfEE), 7, 74
Department of Education and Science (DES), 7
Department of Employment, 7
Department of Trade and Industry (DTI), 10, 98, 131
dependency, 81
  ASEAN model, 84–5
Derby University, 10
dilution of scholarship, 148
distance learning, 152
dynamic impact of university research, 48, 51–4
  measuring, 55–7

earnings
  graduate, 85–6
  trends, 21–2

East Midlands region, 71–3
economic change, 89–90
economic development/growth
　impact of university research, 49–52, 53–7
　knowledge societies, intellectual capital and economic growth, 18–35
　new growth theory, 29–31
　processes, 80–1
　regional, *see* regional development
　role of universities in ASEAN countries, 80–92
　theory, 53–4
　universities and economic growth, 86–7
economic engines, 8–10
economic impact of universities, 47–65
　dynamic, 48, 51–7
　static, 47–8, 48–51
economic infrastructure, 81–2
economic role of universities, 1–2, 3–17
education
　role of formal education in economic growth, 90–1
　and training, 125–6
educational access, 96–7, 118, 146–7
educational attainment, 146–7
educational stockpiling, 33
employers, 74–6
　see also business/industry; labour market; small and medium sized enterprises
endogenous growth theory, 54
engineering, 110
Enterprise in Higher Education (EHE), 6, 12, 74, 79
entrepreneurial university, 26
entrepreneurship, 67
Environet, 145
European Process Industries Competitiveness Centre (EPICC), 97–101
experience
　real life, 155
　work experience, 77
external engagement, 138
extra-organizational networking, *see* networking

factors of production, 53–4
Faraday Partnerships, 16
first degrees, 6, 155, 156
flexibility in provision, 11–12, 77–8
Florida, R., 40–1
focus, selected, 138–9
focus groups, 100
foreign R&D, 56
foreign trade, 56
France, 23
Fryer Report, 4
funding, 5, 7, 132
　financial cuts, 125, 127
　justifying public investment, 19–22
　from marginal activity, 10–11
　research, 25, 132–3
further education (FE) colleges, 118
Further and Higher Education Act (1992), 107

Gateshead MetroCentre, 106
GDP, 49–51, 53–4, 55–7, 59
GEMISIS programme, 136
generic skills/competencies, 74–6
Gibbons, M., 44
Gini coefficient, 81, 85
global economy
　global-local polarity, 6
　thriving locally, 36–46
　Warwick University links to, 119–20
globalization, aspects of, 42
government
　expenditure on research, 24–5
　justifying public investment, 19–22
　policy, *see* policy
　steering changes to HE, 4, 20–2
graduate earnings, 85–6
graduate retention, 41
gross static impact, 49–50
growth companies, 26

Hall, A., 110
hardware, 51–2
Heseltine, M., 98
HESIN (Higher Education Support for Industry in the North), 95, 104
higher education (HE), 66
　changing scene, 3–4, 15–16, 151
　expansion and new opportunities, 15–16

partnerships with SMEs, 76–9
policy shifts, 20–4, 73–6
sector, 71–6
steering changes to, 4, 20–2
variety within, 71–3
Higher Education Funding Council (HEFC), 14
Higher Education Regional Development Fund (HERDF), 74
Highlands, University of the, 6, 150, 152
human capital, 82–3, 83–4
theory, 22–5
see also academic capitalism
human resource management, 41–2

ideas, 29–30
income distribution, 81, 85
industry, see business/industry
Industry Centre, 105–6
information and communication technologies (ICTs), 38
information revolution, 27–8, 96–7
see also knowledge
information technology (IT), 12–13
IT institute at Salford University, 130
networking at Salford University, 135–7
innovation, 26, 52–3
innovation centres, 114
input-output (I-O) models, 47–8, 49–51
Institute of Education, 118
Institute of Work Psychology, 147
institutional thickness, 39
institutionalist approach, 81
integrated chair, 129–30
integrated graduate development programme, 115
intellectual capital, 151
development of, 9–10, 13–14
knowledge societies, economic growth and, 18–35
Islam, I., 81, 85

Japan, 83–4
jobs, 49–51
see also labour market

Kanter, R.M., 38–9, 42
Kay, J., 29–30
Keele, University of, 5
Kennedy Report, 4
Klang Valley development project, 89
knowledge
accumulation and economic growth, 54
dissemination in learning region, 39, 43
dynamic impact of university research, 51–3, 56, 57
information infrastructure and networking, 135–7
kinds of in the learning economy, 40
network knowledge, 40–2, 43
properties of, 28–9
knowledge communities, 31–2, 33
Knowledge House, 95, 101–2, 104, 106
knowledge societies, 18–35
emergence, 27–8
knowledge work, 28
knowledge workers, 27–8, 29–30, 33
KONVER, 114

labour
new kinds of, 27–8
quality of labour stocks, 23–4
labour market
ASEAN countries, 87
generic skills and SMEs, 74–6
learning region and, 41–2, 43–4
trends, 21–2
Lakes, University of the, 6, 13, 150–7
Lanchester College, 110–11
Lane, R., 28
Lasch, C., 33
learning
community model, 154
community university, 152–4
content and process, 153–4
developments in HE, 76
new ways of learning, 15
re-scoping the university, 12–13, 14–15
learning economy, 40
learning region, 37–45
defining, 40–2
Learning World, 106

Leslie, L., 26
levels of achievement, 155–6
Linc Scheme, 114
local environment, 6, 13
  thriving locally in the global economy, 36–46
  see also community; regional development
Longhirst Hall management centre, 102
Lundvall, B.-Å., 39, 40
Lynton, E., 96, 97

Machlup, F., 28
Malaya, University of, 89
Malaysia, 30, 81, 85–91 *passim*
Malaysian Institute of Management, 83, 88
managed approach to research, 133–5
management
  mission and new ways of, 13–14
  of universities and regional development, 42–5
management education, 87–8, 102, 110
Managing Directors Club, 144
'manufacturing corridor', 112
marginal activity, 10–11
market competition, 20
market failure, 70
marketing, 43–4
Massachusetts Institute of Technology (MIT), 31, 52
masters degree, 155, 156
Materials Forum, 144, 145
Materials Technopole, 144, 145
McMaster University, 52
measuring the economic impact of universities, 47–65
Medilink, 145, 146
metropolitan universities, 96
mission, 13–14
Miyai, J., 83–4
Mohnen, P., 56
Molins, 113
Montréal, Université de, 52
motivation to learn, 154
M.Sc. in process manufacturing management, 99–100
multidisciplinary research institutes, 134
multiple choice, 42

National Committee of Enquiry into Higher Education, *see* Dearing Report
National Council for Educational Technology (NCET), 118
national industrial centre for virtual environments, 137
National Science Foundation, 57
National University of Singapore, 90
negotiated processes, 11–12
net static economic impact, 50–1
network knowledge, 40–2, 43
network society, 28
networking
  EPICC, 100–1
  learning region, 42, 45
  Salford University, 135–7
  Sheffield University, 144–6
New Economic Policy, 88–9
new growth theory, 29–31
new institutional economics, 80–1
'new' universities, 5, 6, 8, 9
North-East England, 95–108
Northern Business Forum, 104
Northumbria, University of, 102–4, 107
Nottingham, University of, 7

OECD, 52, 56
Open University, 152

Parallax, 113
partnerships, *see* collaboration
placements, 77
pluralism, 42
PLUS scheme (Project Link University of Sheffield), 143–4
PLUS SME, 143–4
policy
  Malaysia, 88–9
  shifts and HE, 20–4, 73–6
  and SMEs, 69
  see also government
polytechnics, 5–6, 107, 151
post-experience training, 116–17
primary education, 82
private sector research, 24–5
private universities, 88–9
proactive relationships, 77–8
process industries, 97–101, 108

product life cycle, 81
productivity, 55–7, 58–9, 60–1
Psacharopoulos, G., 89
public investment, justifying, 19–22
purpose of universities, 5–6
  reappraisal of, 13–14
Putnam, R.D., 42

real life experience, 155
Realising our Potential, 124
regional development, 143
  learning region, 36–46
  reconceptualizing, 37–9
  re-scoping the university, 8–10, 13
  spillover effect, 30–2
  see also community; local environment
Regional Development Agencies (RDAs), 74
regional office, University of Sheffield, 141–9
Regional Technology Centre, 104
regression analysis, 55, 58
relationships
  with customers/clients, 10–13
  proactive, 77–8
  see also collaboration
relevance, 138–9
re-scoping the university, 3–17
research, 15
  applied, 8, 11, 52–3, 133
  commercialization of, 26
  compatibility with teaching, 6–8
  dependency in ASEAN region, 84–5
  EPICC and R&D, 100
  expenditure on R&D, 24–5, 49–51, 55–7
  and exploitation of academic capital, 24–5
  funds linked to performance, 132–3
  measuring economic impact of universities, 47–65
  and regional development, 43, 44–5
  Salford University, 127–8, 129, 133–5, 139
  University of Cumbria, 155, 156, 157
  University of Sheffield, 144–6, 147–9
research and graduate college, 134
resource mobility, 42
RETEX, 114

Robbins Report, 103
Roberts, G., 141
Roll, E., 22
Rolls Royce, 116
Rover, 115, 116

Sala-I-Martin, X., 29
Salford Quays industrial centre for virtual environments, 137
Salford University, 5, 8, 9, 123–40
Salford University Industrial Centre (SUIC) Ltd (now Salford University Business Services Ltd), 131
Saskatchewan, University of, 52
Science Park, 112–14, 120
self-employment, 68, 69
Sengupta, J.K., 82
services sector, 87–8
Shattock, M., 110, 111
Sheahan, R., 99
Sheffield Heat and Power, 147
Sheffield University Network for Education in the Community, 146–7
Sheffield University Regional Office, 141–9
Silicon Valley, 31, 32, 52
simultaneity, 42
Singapore, 83, 85–91 *passim*
Singapore Institute of Management, 88
skills
  generic, 74–6
  needs of SMEs, 69–71
Skills and Enterprise Network, 70
Slaughter, S., 26
small and medium sized enterprises (SMEs), 66–71, 114
  agenda, 71
  ASEAN region, 89–90
  concerns and skills needs, 69–71
  Knowledge House, 101–2
  partnerships with HE, 76–9
  policy and, 69
  Sheffield University PLUS SME, 143–4
  SME Centre at Warwick Business School, 114, 117
  SME sector, 67–9

software, 51-2, 54
South-East Asia, 30, 80-92
spillover effect, 30-2
Stanford University 31, 52
static economic impact of universities, 47-8, 48-51
Statistics Canada I-O Model, 49-51, 61-2
STEP (Shell Technology and Enterprise Programme), 71, 77, 114
Storey, Professor, 114
Sunderland, University of, 104-6, 107
supply chain, 43

teacher education, 117-18
teaching, 15, 43, 127-8
  compatibility with research, 6-8
  developments in HE, 76
TEAMSTART, 114
technology, 38
  clusters, 31, 52
  economic growth and, 53-4, 56
technology and skill transfer, 127-8
technology transfer, 78, 85, 86, 117
Teesside, University of, 10, 95-102, 107
Teesside Development Corporation, 98
Thatcher, M., 98, 125
Thompson, E., 111
Three Rivers regional strategy, 99
Thrift, N., 39
tiger miracle, 84
time, 148
Todd Commission, 110
total factor productivity (TFP), 56-7, 58-9

training, education and, 125-6
Training and Enterprise Councils (TECs), 70, 102
Trimdon 2000 project, 97
2+2 degree, 118

United States (USA), 21-2, 23, 25, 32
University College Stockton, 16
University Grants Council (UGC), 110
University for Industry (UfI), 156
University of Teesside Partnership, 96
USER (University of Sunderland Environmental Report), 105

vacancies, excess demand for, 74-6
validating bodies, 11
values, Asian, 80, 83
virtual environments, 137
vocationalism, 6, 8

Warwick, University of, 8, 9, 109-22
Warwick Arts Centre, 119
Warwick Business School, 116-17, 120
Warwick Manufacturing Group (WMG), 115-16, 119-20
Warwick Science Park, 112-14, 120
Warwickshire County Council, 109, 113
waste incineration, 147
West Report, 20
wetware, 51-2, 54
Williams, E.T., 110
Wilson, H., 109, 125
Wingspread Group, 21
work experience, 77
World Bank, 81, 82-3, 85

The Society for Research into Higher Education

The Society for Research into Higher Education exists to stimulate and coordinate research into all aspects of higher education. It aims to improve the quality of higher education through the encouragement of debate and publication on issues of policy, on the organization and management of higher education institutions, and on the curriculum and teaching methods.

The Society's income is derived from subscriptions, sales of its books and journals, conference fees and grants. It receives no subsidies, and is wholly independent. Its individual members include teachers, researchers, managers and students. Its corporate members are institutions of higher education, research institutes, professional, industrial and governmental bodies. Members are not only from the UK, but from elsewhere in Europe, from America, Canada and Australasia, and it regards its international work as among its most important activities.

Under the imprint *SRHE & Open University Press*, the Society is a specialist publisher of research, having over 70 titles in print. The Editorial Board of the Society's Imprint seeks authoritative research or study in the above fields. It offers competitive royalties, a highly recognizable format in both hardback and paperback and the worldwide reputation of the Open University Press.

The Society also publishes *Studies in Higher Education* (three times a year), which is mainly concerned with academic issues, *Higher Education Quarterly* (formerly *Universities Quarterly*), mainly concerned with policy issues, *Research into Higher Education Abstracts* (three times a year), and *SRHE News* (four times a year).

The Society holds a major annual conference in December, jointly with an institution of higher education. In 1995 the topic was 'The Changing University' at Heriot-Watt University in Edinburgh. In 1996 it was 'Working in Higher Education' at University of Wales, Cardiff and in 1997, 'Beyond the First Degree' at the University of Warwick. The 1998 conference was on the topic of globalization at the University of Lancaster.

The Society's committees, study groups and networks are run by the members. The networks at present include:

Access	Mentoring
Curriculum Development	Vocational Qualifications
Disability	Postgraduate Issues
Eastern European	Quality
Funding	Quantitative Studies
Legal Education	Student Development

Benefits to members

Individual

Individual members receive

- *SRHE News*, the Society's publications list, conference details and other material included in mailings.
- Greatly reduced rates for *Studies in Higher Education* and *Higher Education Quarterly*.
- A 35 per cent discount on all SRHE & Open University Press publications.
- Free copies of the Precedings – commissioned papers on the theme of the Annual Conference.
- Free copies of *Research into Higher Education Abstracts*.
- Reduced rates for the annual conference.
- Extensive contacts and scope for facilitating initiatives.
- Free copies of the *Register of Members' Research Interests*.
- Membership of the Society's networks.

Corporate

Corporate members receive:

- Benefits of individual members, plus.
- Free copies of *Studies in Higher Education*.
- Unlimited copies of the Society's publications at reduced rates.
- Reduced rates for the annual conference.
- The right to submit applications for the Society's research grants.
- The right to use the Society's facility for supplying statistical HESA data for purposes of research.

Membership details: SRHE, 3 Devonshire Street, London WIN 2BA, UK. Tel: 0171 637 2766. Fax: 0171 637 2781. email:srhe@mailbox.ulcc.ac.uk
World Wide Web:http://www.srhe.ac.uk./srhe/
Catalogue: SRHE & Open University Press, Celtic Court, 22 Ballmoor, Buckingham MK18 1XW. Tel: 01280 823388. Fax: 01280 823233. email:enquiries@openup.co.uk